MARK:
The way for all nations

Cover Photo

Eastern Mennonite College students on Jerusalem Term observe sunrise over the Sea of Galilee. Photo courtesy of Daryl Witmer, Orrville, Ohio.

The Sea of Galilee locates the beginning of the *way* of discipleship in Mark's Gospel. Galilee also functions as Palestine's open door to the *nations*. Like the sunrise, the gospel of Jesus Christ promises a new day for the whole world.

MARK: The way for all nations

Willard M. Swartley

Foreword by Robert P. Meye

HERALD PRESS
Scottdale, Pennsylvania
Kitchener, Ontario

Library of Congress Cataloging in Publication Data

Swartley, Willard M   1936-
   Mark, the way for all nations.

   Bibliography: p.
   1. Bible. N.T. Mark—Study. I. Title.
BS2586.S95   226'.3'06   78-27917
ISBN 0-8361-1883-9 pbk.

MARK: THE WAY FOR ALL NATIONS
Copyright © 1979, 1981 by Herald Press, Scottdale, Pa. 15683
   Published simultaneously in Canada by Herald Press,
   Kitchener, Ont. N2G 4M5
Library of Congress Catalog Card Number: 78-27917
International Standard Book Number: 0-8361-1977-0
Printed in the United States of America
Design: Alice B. Shetler

91 90 89 88 87 86 10 9 8 7 6 5 4 3

To
HOWARD H. CHARLES
who taught me
the inductive method of
Bible study.

Contents

Part II: The Kingdom Way

Part III: The Temple for All Nations

Epilogue

---

*Chorics, used by permission from the companion volume to these studies, *To Walk in the Way,* by Urie A. Bender (Herald Press, 1979). The numbers in parentheses locate the chorics in Bender's book.

Author's Preface

I am indebted to many people for the Bible study method and the insights into Mark's Gospel found in this book. I mention specifically Howard H. Charles, Robert P. Meye, and numerous students whose questions triggered new insights and made the study of Mark exhilarating and enjoyable. I am grateful to Urie Bender for his excellent companion volume consisting of dramatic interpretations of Mark's Gospel. Both his book, *To Walk in the Way,* and mine owe much to the invitation of the Mennonite Church for me to present Bible studies on Mark at its biennial Assembly at Estes Park in June 1977.

In addition to the many persons to whom I am indebted in this rich pilgrimage of stimulation and learning, I am grateful also to the facilitators of this writing project— the Bible study group at Estes Park, especially Dr. George Mark and John Paul Oyer for proposing a free-will offering to pay for time to write, and to the Board of Congregational Ministries (especially Harold Bauman) which took initiative in transcribing the presentations. I express appreciation also to those at Eastern Mennonite College who assisted in the typing (Sharon Swartz Maust during the earlier dissertation stage, Lila Collins, Marie Shenk, Beverly Althouse, Beth Cassel, Rachel Gerber, Sue Hershberger, Priscilla Moser, and

Louisa Swartley) and especially to Mary Swartley, for both her typing of the final copy and encouragement in the project.

For the preparation of the indices in this second printing I thank Mary Jean Kraybill, whose patience, wisdom and care in this project make the book more useful to all of us. Also to Mary Jean Kraybill and Priscilla Stuckey Kauffman I am most grateful for assistance in proofreading to correct errors in the first printing and to give counsel on some of the revisions made in this edition.

Lastly, I am grateful to Herald Press, especially book editor, Paul M. Schrock, for assistance in the final stage of the manuscript and for its publication in this present form.

Willard M. Swartley
Elkhart, Indiana
Revised Edition, February 1981

Foreword

It is a pleasure to commend to future readers this volume with its fruitful combination of historical scholarship joined to Christian devotion, patient observation joined to imaginative application, and sober discipline joined to joyful freedom. Willard Swartley surely demonstrates in this book his gift of teaching. I am sure that the exercise of his gift will lead to the edification of the saints in accordance with 1 Corinthians 14:26. Although the contents of *Mark: The Way for All Nations* will surely stand on their own merits, I am pleased to point out aspects of the work which, for various reasons, attracted my attention.

First of all, Swartley has most profitably further explored and amplified themes which we once considered together. Willard was a member of a most delightful and fruitful class on Mark in the summer school program of Garrett Theological Seminary (now Garrett Evangelical Divinity School) in the summer of 1964. In that course I found myself pursuing (among other matters) the analysis of Markan structure beyond my own basic work in *Jesus and the Twelve,* the initial draft of which was completed in the winter of 1961-62.

By now studies of structure in the Markan narrative are legion. The present study wisely recognizes the possibilities of identifying structural elements without becoming overly dog-

matic regarding such hypotheses. A variety of structural patterns present themselves in Mark—which suggests that the
gospel is rooted in history, the history of God with man,
where the freedom of the Spirit and the surprises of grace
simply defy hardened analysis, both in prospect and in ret-
rospect. There is too little room for grace in too many recent
studies—but not so in this book.

In the second place, I appreciate the way in which the
author underlines the truthful reality of the dictum found in
Mark 4—that the measure you give will be the measure you
get (Mark 4:24). This book was written for students willing to
discipline themselves to learn from Mark; the author knows
how to facilitate the learning encounter. His writing is
interesting and clear. The points of emphasis are faithful to
Mark and the gospel which begot Mark, and Swartley skill-
fully uses a variety of processes to press home the lessons to
be learned. Each unit is preceded by questions which help the
student of Mark to find his/her own way. The exposition
commands attention. It is followed by reflective questions
which multiply the impact of the main content. The footnotes
carry the eager learner ever further into the mysteries of
Mark. And then the recurrent prayers and the succession of
choric materials constantly remind one that Mark is no ordinary history.

Third, I would draw attention to the author's presump-
tion (see the first chapter) that the Evangelist who stands behind the Gospel of Mark is that Mark who is found in the
company of Peter and Paul in the New Testament. If Mark
was the companion of these two great pioneers of the church,
this has profound implications for our thinking about Mark.
I am in agreement with the thesis and appreciate the fact that
it is strongly displayed right off in the first chapter. Theses
with far less real support are often granted far more authority
in shaping arguments about the New Testament. When Mark
is seen as a companion of Peter and Paul in this way, then one

is encouraged to think more directly about the churchly dimensions of Mark.

Finally, the book is willing to ask questions without always seeking to answer them. The Gospel of Mark is like that—and there is no reason to believe that we can outrun the second evangelist. I am thankful for the present study and hope that the author will continue to share his findings and his questions with those who seek to be disciples in the way of the cross.

Robert P. Meye, Dean
Fuller Theological Seminary
Pasadena, California
Thanksgiving, 1978

Introduction

During the last nineteen centuries the Gospel of Mark has had a checkered history of influence within the Christian church. This history may be described in five stages.

1. *A Gospel for the Church.* Whether Mark was the first Gospel written (as most scholars hold) or the last of the Synoptics (as a growing minority holds), it is clear that Mark wrote his Gospel to serve the needs of the church in the late sixties or early seventies. The Gospel shows Jesus as the Messiah of the cross, calling Christians to live the servant life and to follow Jesus on the way that leads to suffering, the cross, and the kingdom of God. The kingdom, which Jesus brought with him, calls also for mission to the Gentiles, whom Mark strikingly includes in the Gospel's narrative. In addition to these themes, Mark stresses the eschatological urgency of the kingdom message, the secrecy and disclosure of Jesus' identity, and the rejection of Jesus' messiahship by the Jewish leaders.[1]

As this study will indicate, Mark wrote his story of Jesus to anchor the proclamation of the gospel among the Gentiles in the history of Jesus and Judaism. As a mediating figure between the Petrine and the Pauline communities, Mark's thirty years of experience in early Christian history put him in a unique and authoritative position to write a distinctive account of the gospel-story, a Gospel that gained acceptance by the church.

2. *Lectionary for the Christian Year.* Perhaps because Mark's Gospel is the shortest of the four canonical Gospels, in the third and fourth centuries it apparently came to be used as a lectionary for weekly readings in early Christian worship. Philip Carrington has pointed out that Codex Vaticanus (B), an important fourth-century manuscript, has the Gospel of Mark divided into forty-eight sections. When scheduled on the civil or agricultural years these sections correlate well with the events of the Jewish-Christian year (several Sundays are assigned to special readings to close the gap between forty-eight and fifty-two readings).[2] While Carrington argues that the Gospel was written originally to function as a lectionary, it is commonly agreed by scholars that the sectional divisions of Codex Vaticanus were added in the early centuries. This suggests that for several centuries at least, the Gospel of Mark played an influential role in some of the early Christian communities.

3. *The Lesser Influence.* It appears, however, that the Gospel of Mark receded into a place of lesser influence in the church as preference for the other three Gospels developed. With the development of papal (Petrine) authority in Christendom and the established character of Christianity, the Gospel of Matthew with its distinctively positive portraits of Peter emerged into foremost influence, both liturgically and catechetically. Luke, with its longer text and special sections of Jesus' teachings, contributed additional material for the church's nurture. The Gospel of John provided its own spiritual understanding of the life and ministry of Jesus.[3] It appears, therefore, that the Gospel of Mark played a lesser role within the Christian church during the medieval and reformation centuries.

But to this there were exceptions. The Coptic church in Egypt, tracing its origin to Mark's missionary work in Egypt, continued to hold Mark's Gospel in preeminence, likely both as a lectionary source and a catechetical guide (see Appendix

I, B). The tradition that Mark's body was stolen from Egypt
and taken to Venice in AD 827 would also indicate some
Markan influence in the Roman church in Italy.

4. *The Valued Source.* With the development and use of
the historical-critical method in biblical studies in the
eighteenth century, the Gospel of Mark came to be a highly
valued historical source for writing "lives of Jesus" in the
nineteenth century. The so-called Markan hypothesis carried
two significant implications. First, the Gospel of Mark was
now regarded as the earliest Gospel written, contrary to the
view of Matthean priority that had developed in the tradition
of the church in the earlier centuries. This meant that in the
writing of their Gospels, Matthew and Luke used Mark;
Mark was considered the original.

Second, scholars attributed to Mark's Gospel greater
historical reliability. The nineteenth century witnessed a
heady optimism in achieving objective results in historical research. Scholars believed that they could distinguish between
two types of material within the Gospels: the real history of
objective facts and the church's later interpretations. Mark's
Gospel thus often functioned as the "judge" in the decision-
making process since Mark's account was regarded as the
original and the more historically reliable.[4] The longer Gospels of Matthew and Luke appeared to be more interpretive,
secondary, and consequently, according to nineteenth-
century assumptions, less reliable. For biblical scholars during this period of the Western church's history, the Gospel of
Mark functioned as the anchor cast into the sea of early writings on Christian origins.

5. *Purposes of Its Own.* In the early twentieth century,
William Wrede's study of Mark signaled a different understanding for the future of Markan studies. Wrede noticed
that Mark couched Jesus' public ministry within a secrecy
motif. Wrede considered this emphasis to have arisen not
from Jesus' history but from the church's theological effort to

resolve two problems: (1) after his resurrection Jesus became Messiah but during his ministry he was not so perceived—so far as the belief of his followers was concerned, and (2) after Jesus' resurrection and the reception of the Spirit at Pentecost, the disciples acquired a messianic understanding of Jesus but during his earthly ministry they did not perceive him as Messiah. Mark's messianic secret was thus developed by the church as a device to correlate the original non-messianic history of Jesus with the later messianic faith of the church (i.e., the messianic secret both conceals and reveals Jesus' messianic identity).[5] Although this view has not stood among Markan scholars, the last twenty years have vindicated Wrede's approach in that Markan scholars now agree that the Gospel is indeed toned with theological purposes and distinctive literary intentions.

The earlier studies in this past twenty-year period sought to identify redactional (or editorial) emphases of Mark as author. Scholars attempted to distinguish between the tradition received by Mark and the special emphases which he contributed to the text, either by minor additions or modifications, by providing seams that hold together the various traditions he received, or by his distinctive arrangement of the material.[6] Since it was assumed that Mark was written first, it was difficult for scholars to achieve consensus on their findings because it was not possible to compare Mark's text with an earlier written source.[7]

In the last decade, Markan studies have moved in the direction of identifying various literary elements within the narrative of the Gospel.[8] These studies have yielded a rich variety of understandings and insights, many of which support one another.

A prominent weakness in these contributions, however, has been restrictiveness in scope. Many studies are an intensive analysis of one or several chapters only. What emerges as the distinctive emphasis of that part of the Gospel is then either too quickly taken as the key to the whole Gospel, not related to the remaining parts of the Gospel, or correlated only inferentially with themes developed from other studies on other parts of the text.

In this context of need, this study seeks to understand how all the parts of the Gospel fit together into one literary whole. It is not, however, an intensive scholarly study of any particular part of the Gospel, nor is it written primarily for scholars. However, its insights build upon the more scholarly study of my dissertation, *A Study in Markan Structure: The Influence of Israel's Holy History upon the Structure of the Gospel of Mark.*

This study of Mark's Gospel follows the literary method; it is described best perhaps as compositional analysis.[9] The inductive method of Bible study (see Appendix II, B) has significantly influenced my use of the literary method. But my approach has also been enriched greatly by methods and perceptions contributed by redactional studies, narrative analysis, and structuralist studies.[10]

Of highest priority among the goals of this book, I wish to present a study of the Gospel which catches up the readers in the learning process. First, it is a resource for studying the Gospel; second, it is a book of findings. The reader may not agree with all the findings. In fact, the reader may discover other insights through the process of study. This is as it should be. For the goal of this volume is to introduce people eager for Bible study to a fruitful and current approach to the study of the Gospels.

Suggestions for Using This Book

This book is written for either individual or group study of Mark's Gospel. If it is used for group study, the teacher-leader should work ahead of the group and seek to draw from the group members their insights. The group should focus its study upon the assigned text in Mark and limit its use of this book to the presession questions at the beginning of each chapter while the teacher-leader should work through the entire chapter scheduled for study. Many groups will find they need two sessions for each chapter, one session to share learnings from the *presession study* and a second to discuss the *exposition* and the *reflection, discussion and action* sections of the same chapter.

Each chapter contains four parts or phases of study. These are:

1. The *presession study*. This consists of questions to help the reader develop a method of study (see Appendix II, B) and to guide the reader to important observations leading to the interpreting of the text. Even when the book is used individually (as most books are read), taking time to study the biblical text and working through the presession questions will greatly enrich the learning.

2. The *exposition*. The exposition is my commentary on the Markan text. In group study, the leader after reading the

exposition should seek to lead the group to the key insights through questions and discussion. The leadership function may rotate among members in the group, thus drawing more people into the excitement of participating in both sides of the learning process. Each exposition ends with a prayer which seeks to identify the growth-edge to which the biblical text calls us.

3. *A visual portrayal of the study* in the form of a structural diagram. This diagram seeks to summarize and provide photographic recall of the main points learned about the text. Usually there is space below the diagram to write additional observations and notes.

4. *A discussion, reflection, and action* section. This consists of comments and questions whose purpose is twofold: to reinforce the crucial learnings (sometimes with supplementary insights) and to raise questions which apply or correlate the studies to our contemporary situations. The leader of the study group may request certain members of the group to prepare in advance a brief statement on each discussion issue. The function of this statement might be (a) to focus the issue toward a local context so that the study group can immediately see its pertinence, (b) to amplify the issue to include other dimensions (for example, biblical considerations outside Mark's Gospel), or (c) to contribute additional practical considerations.

The best way to study the Bible is to do it. *Bon voyage* with God's guidance.

How to Use

To Walk in the Way

With This Study

Dramatic interpretations of Mark's Gospel, written by Urie A. Bender, and published in a companion volume to this book, may be used in conjunction with the chapters of this study as follows:

Swartley's	Bender's
Mark: The Way For All Nations	*To Walk in the Way*
Throughout	There Is a Way: Choric
Chapter 1	Mark Introduces Jesus
Chapter 2	Early Conflict—Jesus and the Pharisees
Chapter 3	Secrets Are for Telling
Chapters 4 (5)	Hints of Identity
Chapter 6	Declaration and Unveiling
Chapter 7	The Greatest Is Servant of All
Chapter 8	To Choose or Not to Choose the Way
Chapter 9	Later Conflict—Jesus and the Pharisees
Chapter 10	No Curtain Now
Chapter 11	Finale—The Servant Died on the Way to Exaltation

(handwritten: 12-21-86)

I am grateful to Urie A. Bender for giving me permission to include seven of his shorter pieces in this volume. These chorics are noted in the Table of Contents. I trust these will lead you to his volume of many more rich resources, *To Walk in the Way* (Herald Press, 1979).

PROLOGUE

Chapter 1

John Mark: Deserter for the Church

Presession Study

Learn as much as you can about John Mark, the author of the Gospel of Mark.

1. What was John Mark's role in the early church? Read Acts 13:1-13 and 15:36-40. Why did John Mark go home? What is the meaning of the word "minister" (or helper) in Acts 13:5? Compare Luke 1:2. Why did John Mark go along with Barnabas and Saul? Can you see any connection between the dispute at the Jerusalem Conference and Paul's dissension with Barnabas over John Mark, both occurring in Acts 15?

2. Note John Mark's role later on in the early church. Read Colossians 4:10; 2 Timothy 4:11-13; and 1 Peter 5:13. Why the parenthetical statement in Colossians 4:10? Was Mark helping *both* Paul and Peter in these years around AD 62-65?

3. Do you know anything about John Mark prior to the first missionary journey, that is, from Acts, chapters 1—12? Do you see any possible connection between chapter 1 and chapter 12?

4. In Mark's Gospel itself, do you find any information that might tell us something about John Mark? What about 14:51, 52?

5. How many years are covered by these various snapshots of the life of John Mark? When did he write the Gospel? What about the "books and the parchments" in 2 Timothy 4:11-13?

EXPOSITION

*John Mark's Role in the Early Church's Missionary
Movement (AD 47-50)*

Who was John Mark? Most of us think immediately of
the young man who deserted Barnabas and Paul on the first
missionary journey. John Mark was a quitter, we say. He
couldn't take the stress and uncertainties of missionary life.

But are we sure about this? The biblical text doesn't tell
us specifically why he went home. Remember that John Mark
also wrote a Gospel, possibly the first Gospel to be widely
used and accepted as authoritative by the church. Perhaps his
reasons for going home were quite responsible and even
praiseworthy. At least we should examine all available evidence and make as fair a judgment as possible.

Some commentators have suggested that John Mark
went home to care for his ailing mother. One writer manages
to get in a romantic touch: he went home to see his girl-
friend? My response: "Romantic indeed, but not likely."

The true reason for John Mark's desertion is certainly more
serious. What is clear from the biblical text is that Paul, in the
early stage of his missionary work (Acts 15:36-40), evaluated
John Mark negatively. But at a later date (Colossians 4:10; 2
Timothy 4:11), Paul highly valued John Mark's company and
contribution. This chapter will seek to reconstruct, as far as
possible, the course of events that gave rise to both Paul's dissension with Barnabas over John Mark and Paul's later affirmation
of Mark's usefulness to his missionary enterprise.

In order to understand John Mark's role during the earlier
period of Paul's missionary career, five factors need to be
considered:

1. The significance of Mark's role on the first journey. Most
of us know the text which says that "John left them and returned
to Jerusalem" (Acts 13:13). The statement does not say why
Mark deserted Barnabas and Paul on the first missionary

journey. A description of John Mark's role on the first missionary team provides a clue, however, for understanding the significance of Mark's desertion. Verse 5 tells us that John went along with Barnabas and Saul (later called Paul) "to assist them."

That, however, is not an adequate translation. In the Greek text it says they took John along as a *hupēretēs*. What does that mean? The same word is used in Luke 1:2, where Luke tells us that he depended on the eyewitnesses and the ministers *(hupēretai,* plural) of the Word for his information about Jesus. From this text it appears that the *hupēretēs* was an officially recognized authority on the deeds and teachings of Jesus. The use of this term in earlier Greek writings to describe divine messengers who had the power and authority of the gods behind them provided the background for the broader use of this term where it denoted "service of any kind which in structure and goal is controlled by the will of him to whom it is rendered." [1]

Significant studies have also been done on the methods by which the Jewish community passed on its teachings by oral transmission during the early centuries BC and AD. These studies show that specific pupils *(talmid)* were selected to memorize the tradition. Those regarded superior in their work not only memorized but also interpreted the oral tradition. [2] To be a "minister of the Word" then was a specific task performed by one who had been trained to memorize and pass on a particular body of knowledge. This, I suggest, was Mark's role on the first missionary journey. [3] As a *hupēretēs,* Mark knew, recited, and possibly interpreted the words and deeds of Jesus. In this role he contributed significantly to the missionary assignment of this first team sent out from Antioch.

2. The different roles of the three men sent on this first journey also merit consideration. Commissioned by the church at Antioch, Syria, the first missionary company sailed to Cyprus (Acts 13:1-4), Barnabas's native country (Acts 4:36). Because he knew the culture and the people, and since his name regularly ap-

pears first in the early part of the journey, Barnabas undoubtedly functioned as the leader of the group as they moved from one city to another in Cyprus. As moderator, he would introduce Saul who in turn told of his marvelous conversion, a call to evangelize all people, including the Gentiles, by the grace of God.

At some point in the service, Barnabas would also introduce John Mark, his relative (Colossians 4:10). He would present John Mark as one taught by the Apostle Peter to memorize and interpret the life and teachings of Jesus Christ.

We learn also that Paul emerged fully into the leadership position upon entering Asia Minor. Notice the name change from Saul to Paul and the reversal of the order of the names (now Paul and Barnabas) from Acts 13:13 onward (except in 14:14). Upon entering the Gentile territory of Asia Minor, the country of Paul's native Tarsus, two events occurred simultaneously: John Mark left for home and Paul became the unmistaken leader of the group.

3. A third consideration examines John Mark's relationship to Peter. According to the widespread testimony of the early church from the second to fourth centuries, John Mark received the gospel from Peter (see Appendix I, part A). This substantial evidence suggests that Peter, an apostolic eyewitness, personally trained Mark to be a *hupēretēs*.

It is important to recognize, therefore, that John Mark functioned as a "minister" to both Peter and Paul on the first missionary journey. Upon leaving Paul and Barnabas, Mark returned to Jerusalem, probably went directly to Peter, and reported on the developments of the first journey. In my judgment, Mark's desertion was occasioned by a twofold factor: (1) John Mark had not originally anticipated the taking of the gospel into the Gentile world of Asia Minor; and (2) feeling responsible to Peter and possibly also to "the circumcision party" John Mark returned to Jerusalem to report on Paul's intentions to accept the Gentiles without requiring circumcision. John Mark's return to Jerusalem then was a contributing factor to the Jerusalem Conference.

4. The sequence of events in Acts 15 suggests that the issues of the Jerusalem Conference were connected to the dispute that took place over Barnabas' desire to have John Mark join them on the second journey (Acts 15:36-40). I suggest the following scenario: since the church had approved the acceptance of Gentiles without circumcision, Barnabas felt Mark should now rejoin the team; the problem that occasioned his desertion was now settled. But Paul, unable to forget the hurt of Mark's desertion, objected vigorously. Even a "sharp contention" produced no compromise.

That Paul was especially sensitive to the authority of the Jerusalem "pillars" is quite clear (Galatians 2:1-10 likely parallels Acts 15). A conflict between Paul and Peter, reported in Galatians 2:11-14, indicates that Paul did not feel Peter fully accepted the Gentiles within the church community. Although Peter himself supported the Gentile mission, as his role in Acts 10-11 and Acts 15:1-11 indicates, he nonetheless felt the influence of the more conservative "circumcision party." Even Acts 10-11 does not indicate clearly that the baptism of Cornelius and other Gentiles did not need to be supplemented by circumcision. If that issue had been decided before the first journey, the Jerusalem Conference would have been unnecessary.

5. Paul's passionate commitment to bring the Gentiles into the Christian community *without circumcision* was rooted in the call that he received during his Damascus Road experience (Acts 9; 22; 26). That call linked the acceptance of Jesus as the Messiah to the mission to the Gentiles. For Paul, the meaning of Jesus' messiahship was the proclamation of the age of fulfillment, the time when the Gentiles were to come into the kingdom of God as Gentiles, thus fulfilling the eschatological vision of numerous Old Testament prophecies (see, for example, Isaiah 56:6-8).

John Mark felt loyalty in both directions. He understood the teachings of Jesus well enough to know that they pointed in the direction of including outsiders, even Gentiles, but, having grown up in Jerusalem and having been trained, like Peter, to regard the Gentiles as unclean, Mark felt strong loyalties also to the Jerusalem brethren who wanted to preserve Judaism within Christianity.

In the context of these five considerations, we can better understand the significance of John Mark's desertion on the first missionary journey. We can also understand why Paul did not want to take him along again when he had already shown loyalty, to the point of desertion, to the authority of the Jerusalem church. Certainly Paul did not want another Jerusalem Conference after his second journey. But Paul did take along another representative from the Jerusalem church, Silas, whom Paul chose (15:40). Although Silas was a leading man among the Jerusalem brethren (15:22), we have no evidence that he could function as a *huperetēs* in the same way that John Mark did, although the possibility is not excluded.

While this interpretation of John Mark's return to Jerusalem may appear to ignore the explicit statement of the text—because he "had not gone with them to the work" (Acts 15:38b), it in fact does not. (This statement does not say *why* he left. To say that he became tired or gave up is also a suggested reason for why he didn't go with them to the work.)

What was "the work" in the shadow of Acts 15? Was it not the Gentile mission—the precise issue that necessitated the Jerusalem conference? It is noteworthy that *The International Standard Bible Encyclopedia* (written already in 1929) says:

> Why did he [John Mark] turn back from the work [Acts 13:13]? Not because of homesickness, or anxiety for his mother's safety, or home duties, or the desire to rejoin Peter, or fears of the perils incident to the journey, but rather because he objected to the offer of salvation to the Gentiles on condition of faith alone. There are hints that M.'s family, like Paul's, were Hebrew of the Hebrews. . . . [4]

This reconstruction of events must remain an hypothesis, but a plausible one in my judgment. It explains why such a sharp disagreement arose between Paul and Barnabas; it puts Mark's desertion during the first journey in a credible light; it fits well with what we learn elsewhere about Paul's relation to Jerusalem (Galatians 1:18—2:15), as well as Mark's relation to Peter; and it becomes a strategic piece in the mosaic of John Mark's later career, which we are about to examine.

John Mark's Role in the Later Church's Missionary Movement (AD 60-65)

The story continues. Later on, John Mark was valued highly by both Paul and Peter. I propose that John Mark was functioning behind the scenes, helping to keep these two powerful figures in the early church together, and to keep the church one church.

Several texts written during this later period are pertinent. Colossians 4:10 reads: "Aristarchus my fellow prisoner greets you, and Mark the cousin of Barnabas (concerning whom you have received instructions—if he comes to you, receive him)." That's an interesting parenthetical phrase. Paul, writing to the church at Colossae, says, "If this man John Mark comes along, concerning whom I have already sent special instructions, he's all right. Receive him!"

This part of the early church apparently knew that Paul and Barnabas had had a tiff over John Mark earlier on. "For indeed, there was no small dissension." Now, however, here in Colossians around AD 62, about fifteen years later, John Mark's all right. "If he comes, receive him."

Look also in 2 Timothy 4:11: "Luke alone is with me. Get Mark and bring him with you; for he is very useful in serving me." *Paul* says, "This man John Mark is very useful in serving me." And then in verses 12 and 13, Paul adds (and I'm always fascinated by these verses), "Tychicus I have sent

to Ephesus. When you come, bring the cloak that I left with
Carpus at Troas, also the books, and above all the parchments."

How interesting that Paul says, Mark is useful to me and
I want the books and the parchments. What's really going on
here when Paul is in prison about AD 62-65? Is this the time
when John Mark is writing his Gospel? Is that why John
Mark is useful and why the books and the parchments must
come along?

It could well be. What a possibility!

Look now in 1 Peter 5:13. To the best of our knowledge,[5]
both Paul and Peter were in prison in Rome during this period and Peter writes, "She who is at Babylon . . . sends you
greetings; and so does "my son Mark." Read the quotations
from the early church fathers (Appendix I, Part A); these are
in solid agreement that Mark received the content for his
Gospel from Peter.

What's shaping up here in AD 62-65? It appears, does it
not, that John Mark is performing a service that is valuable
to both Paul and Peter? This situation provides the setting for
an important question: How was John Mark in a position to
write this Gospel for the Christian movement? How was he
recognized as one who could write a Gospel with the result
that it was approved and accepted by the church?

Many gospels were written (Luke 1:1) and many were
not accepted by the church. How did John Mark, guided by
God and the Spirit, write a Gospel that was accepted by the
church and accorded canonical status? Mark's Gospel functioned at the center of the Christian movement. Who was this
man John Mark? We need to know more about him.

To recapitulate, our first glimpse of John Mark's role in
the early church took us to the period AD 47-50, during the
first missionary journey. The second glimpse took us to the
end of Paul's life, AD 62-65, when Paul and Peter were both
in prison.

John Mark's Association with the Church in Jerusalem
Prior to AD 45

But do we know anything about John Mark prior to this time? Look in Acts 12:12. According to this text, John Mark lived in Jerusalem in the home of his mother, Mary. To that house Peter went after he got out of prison. Peter knew where the apostles would be assembled, so he went there—to the home of John Mark! This glimpse into Mark's life takes us to the time period of AD 40-45.

But might there be a connection to an earlier period? Is this house the same house mentioned in Acts 1:12-14? Is this the house that contained the upper room where the apostles went after the resurrection and the ascension? If these two houses (in Acts 1:12 and 12:12 where the apostles gathered in both instances) are the same, then John Mark not only lived in, but likely also grew up in the house in Jerusalem that contained the upper room. This is an important third stage in the history of John Mark.

John Mark's Association with Jesus (AD 28, 29)

Let's push back one step still further and ask, What do we know about this man even prior to Acts 1:12-14? Do we have any knowledge of John Mark from Jesus' own lifetime? Such information would come, likely, from the Gospel itself. Does Mark in his Gospel tell us anything about himself? Many commentators suggest that chapter 14, verses 51 and 52, may refer to John Mark. This event—in which the young man lost his clothes—occurred during the night of Jesus' arrest in the Garden of Gethsemane.

We've heard sermons about the way all the disciples forsook Jesus during that night (and it is true!). Nonetheless, this one young man lingered on in the garden. Perhaps he hid behind bushes watching what would happen to Jesus. Suddenly, a soldier saw him and caught hold of him. But the young man managed to slip out of his clothes and escape completely naked. Out of faithfulness to Jesus, this young man risked his life and lost his clothes.

The story is not finished. Some commentators have suggested that the "man" mentioned in 14:13 might be the same as the "young man" in 14:51. Jesus sends two of his disciples into the city and tells them that a man will meet them who, oddly, will be carrying a pitcher of water on his head (a job done only by women). He will take them to a room where they should prepare the Last Supper.

Whether this "man" should be identified with the "young man" in the garden is uncertain. The two occurrences of "young man" in the RSV text (14:51; 16:5) translate the Greek word *neaniskos,* but the word in 14:13 is *anthrōpos,* the normal word for man. Only if the meeting place of Acts 12:12 is identified with the upper room of Acts 1:12 is there reason to think that the "man" in Mark 14:13 is John Mark (since then the "man," John Mark, is going to his home). If these two scenes in the early Christian story are located in John Mark's home, then John Mark is associated with the Last Supper, perhaps assisting in serving the meal (and overhearing some of the conversation).

Although these suggested identifications of John Mark with the upper room events must remain doubtful, or at least not certain, the second occurrence of *neaniskos* in Mark's Gospel takes us to a scene in which the "young man's" role astounds us. Like the women in the Easter narrative, we are inclined to run away, filled with fear and amazement! Look at 16:5—but hold on to your seats as you read! Whom did the women find in the tomb? A *neaniskos,* the same word as in 14:51, "a young man!"

That almost "blows our minds!" In the tomb on Easter morning we meet, first of all, "a young man." Now I know that Matthew and John refer to an angel or angels in the tomb but that's really not a problem because, as in the Old Testament, a human person may be transformed into an angel, or an angel may appear in human form.[6] An angel (in Hebrew, *malak*) is simply a messenger of God.[7]

May I push the point a bit further into a little homily for our edification. Is it possible that in God's grace and providence the young man who lost his clothes for the sake of the kingdom on Good Friday eve received new heavenly clothes on Easter morning?—that in that glorious and triumphant moment he was transfigured and transformed by the grace of God![8]

During these studies of Mark's Gospel, I want you to think about the tremendous contribution Mark has made to Christian believers through the ages in the writing of this Gospel. Think also carefully and seriously about this man's role in the life of the early church in both his younger and older years, his possible first encounters with Jesus (AD 28, 29), his association with the Jerusalem apostles who met in his home (AD 30-47), his role during Paul's first missionary journey (AD 47-50), and, finally, his assistance to both Paul and Peter while they were in prison (AD 60-65).

Further, if we accept the testimony from the church fathers about the Coptic Church in Egypt, we learn that John Mark first brought the gospel to Egypt (see Appendix I, Part B). In its liturgy, the Coptic Church today honors Saint Mark as its apostle, evangelist, and martyr. Indeed, there seems to be a lot more going for John Mark than we often give him and God credit for.

In view of this, I propose that John Mark held a unique position in the early church, that his position was so recognized both in Jerusalem and throughout the Gentile world, and that he indeed was the proper person to write this "Gospel of Jesus Christ." Though he left for home during the first missionary journey, he deserted for the sake of the church's unity. Mark functioned as a bridge between Peter and Paul. Linked to Peter through his training as a *hupēretēs* of the gospel and linked to Paul in the cause of the Gentile mission, Mark wrote the Gospel to win Gentiles into the kingdom of God, a cause which Peter, by the direction of God's Spirit, came also to support firmly.

The Gospel itself has dramatic features, as we will find in these studies. It is a disclosure of Jesus' personhood, who he is, and how that is to be understood. The Gospel declares that Jesus knew the way of the cross. One commentator has called the Gospel of Mark the Gospel of the Way, and indeed Mark makes a point of this term, as we shall see later when we study Mark 8—10. Mark is the only Gospel to associate two Old Testament prophetic texts which contain this crucial term "way." Mark alone puts them together and with these he begins his Gospel of the Way, the Gospel of Jesus Christ, the Son of God:

> "As it is written in Isaiah the prophet,
> 'Behold, I send my messenger before thy face,
> who shall prepare the *way;*
> the voice of one crying in the wilderness:
> Prepare the *way* of the Lord,
> make his paths straight—' " (italics mine)[9]

O Lord,
   we have been in touch with your work,
      with the drama of your gospel-history.
Though separated by centuries and miles,
   we feel kinship with the
      Evangelist, John Mark.
We thank you, Lord,
   for his role in the kingdom—
      for his willingness to be trained by Peter,
      for his openness to be used by Paul,
      for his patience to work with both.
We thank you for the Gospel he wrote.

As we take up this study,
   let the good news
      make us new.
May the Jesus of this Gospel become
   our Savior and
   our Lord.
                        Amen.

Reflection, Discussion, and Action

1. Jack Finegan has written a most interesting book of historical fiction on John Mark entitled, *Mark of the Taw* (Atlanta: John Knox Press, 1972). The book reflects most of the points made in this chapter and includes others as well. If possible, have someone report on the book before this session.

2. Have you felt the impact of this chapter's thesis on early church history? If one imagines a continuum of positions in the early church on accepting Gentiles into the church without circumcision, where would you put the following persons or groups on the continuum? The circumcision party (Acts 15:1)? Paul? Peter? James (Acts 15:13-21)? Barnabas? John Mark? Read Galatians 2.

3. Can you imagine what the history of the Christian church would have been like had there developed in AD 50 a Paul-denomination (with uncircumcised Gentiles in) and a Pro-circumcision denomination (with uncircumcised Gentiles out)? To what extent do you think John Mark by God's power and grace kept this from happening? Notice also Barnabas' role (Acts 9:27; 15:2 and Galatians 2:13)!

4. What can this study teach us about the role of "behind-the-scenes" figures in the life of the church today? Do we perhaps see only the Pauls and the Peters and overlook the John Marks? How important was Mark's Gospel to the early church—to both Jewish and Gentile Christians?

5. Study Paul's teaching on spiritual gifts for Christian ministry (Romans 12:3-8; Ephesians 4:7, 11-14; 1 Corinthians 12:4-11, 27-31). Which gifts do you think John Mark had?

6. Elizabeth O'Connor's book, *Eighth Day of Creation* (Waco: Word Books, 1971), assists Christians in discerning and affirming each other's gifts. Perhaps you'll want to put this on your study agenda after you complete this study.

7. Are there any differences of positions in your group or congregation which a John Mark type of person can help to bridge? Who in your group has the gifts to fill this role?

There Is a Way

CHORIC

There is a way...
    marked across the geography of time
    ...a torturous way
    ...a joyful way
        at times
        dropping into the valleys of everyday
        mortality;
        at the same time
        transcending body and place,
        and wending
        a heady path
        past the peaks of eternal reality
    glistening
        (in)
    evening's promise
        (of)
    a new day
            ...a way
    which now and then
        is clearly seen
        or suddenly hid from view
        now sharply shaped
        each rocky detail
            and
        twisting form
        stark—
        then (and most often)
        both feet and path
        lost in an earthy haze
so that each step—
    made firmly
    —must be made

in faith.
. . . a way
—marked by one
who has walked it
in
both directions—
marked by one
who
being in the form of God
did not count equality with God
a thing
to be grasped (but)
stripped himself of all privilege

consented
to become
servant
and be born
mortal man
stripped
servant
mortal
(what further humbling
could grace command?)

this one
walked
the way to death. . .
. . . the servant died
on the way
to exaltation
the servant died
on the way
to exaltation

—From *To Walk in the Way*

Part I

WHO IS THIS MAN?

"Who then is this,
that even wind
and sea
obey him?"

Chapter 2

Jesus Bursts Old Wineskins: Religion's Problem with Jesus

(Mark 2:1—3:6)

Presession Study

1. How many separate paragraphs are in this segment, 2:1—3:6? What is the definition of a segment (see Appendix II, Section B)?

2. Make a visual diagram of the segment as follows, showing where each paragraph begins and ends:

```
|2:1                    2:12|2:13              2:17|2:18   etc.|
```

3. Give each paragraph a descriptive title. A descriptive title is not an interpretation; it simply tells what happens in the paragraph. "Jesus Wins the Argument" is *not* a descriptive title for verses 1-12 because it doesn't describe the distinctive action of the paragraph. Rather one such as *Jesus Heals a Paralytic* or *Jesus Forgives the Paralytic's Sins* is a descriptive title. Write the descriptive title in the space above the paragraph line.

4. Take some time to study the summary of the induc-

tive method of Bible study in Appendix II, Section B. Notice the three main parts: Observation, Interpretation, and Application. This study of Mark's Gospel should improve your skills in all three areas. Sound interpretation and meaningful application, however, depend upon good and correct observations. Hence, I will focus especially on different types of observations in this study.

5. Can you identify any "non-routine" key terms in this segment? Make your own list and then compare it with another person's list, if you are studying as a group. As you read the exposition, note the key terms which I select and sometimes define.

6. One of the laws of structural relationship is repetition. Repeated words may indeed be key terms. Can you find any repeated words in the chapter (*not* a, the, and but!)?

7. Do you see any contrasts in the segment? Any comparisons? Any progression? What is the mood or atmosphere of the segment?

8. Can you find the unifying "raw material" of the segment? Perhaps there's more than one answer. Do the following contribute to the unity of the segment?

	Yes	No
a. Persons	____	____
b. Places	____	____
c. Events	____	____
d. Ideas	____	____
e. Time	____	____

At the end of the exposition, I'll share my answer.

9. Record your various observations below the hori-

zontal line diagram that you made for question 2 above.

10. On the interpretive level, what's going on in this segment? What do the terms "Son of man," "Lord of the Sabbath," and the images in verses 19-22 mean?

11. Suggest several interpretive titles for the segment. Find one that reflects the thrust of the entire segment.

12. How do you think this theme should be applied to our present religious situation? If your pastor would preach from this passage, to what specific situations in your church life should he speak?

EXPOSITION: MARK 2:1–3:6

One need not read far in the Gospel until one senses that
Mark writes with dramatic style. Drama is evident especially
in the various responses to Jesus. In Mark's Gospel various
groups of people respond differently to Jesus.

Responses to Jesus
Although the majority of responses to Jesus will be more
fully described in later chapters, a brief overview of the range
of responses, with fuller portraits of a few, may be noted at
this early stage in the Gospel's narrative.
Note first the response of the crowds. Quite frequently,
crowds gather to see what Jesus did. In 1:33, 37, 45, masses of
people press around Jesus. In 2:12 after the healing of the
paralytic, the crowds are amazed, and glorify God, saying,
"We never saw anything like this!" When Jesus comes home,
a crowd gathers, and prevents Jesus from eating (3:20). In 4:1
a large crowd gathers to hear his teaching; in 10:46 a great
multitude accompanies Jesus as he comes into Jericho; and in
11:10 when Jesus rides into Jerusalem, many people cry out,
acclaiming him as the one who brings the Davidic kingdom
that is coming! In all these cases the crowds respond positively. They are amazed and astounded. But their response
has no depth and carries no commitment, as shown finally by
the crowds crying for his crucifixion (15:8-15).
Another type of response to be examined in this chapter,
comes from the Pharisees and other religious leaders.
The third group consists of Jesus' family and friends. In
3:21, Jesus' own family and friends do not know what to make
of him; they say he is beside himself. They conclude that he is
not operating normally because he does not fit the patterns of
normal behavior. In 6:1-6 Jesus' home people reject him.
How hard it must have been for Jesus when those who were
close to him for many years turned against him.

A fourth type of response comes from the disciples. As we proceed through the studies of these chapters, observe carefully what the disciples know about Jesus and how they respond to him in Mark's Gospel.

The fifth and sixth groups are what I'll call the D and D groups. These refer to the divine and the demonic voices. How do the divine and the demonic forces respond to Jesus in the Gospel of Mark? The next chapter will focus on this in the context of discussing the messianic secret in Mark's Gospel.

There is still another group—a *seventh* group—which we will call the outsiders. This includes the sinners, but also especially the Gentiles. How do they respond to Jesus? Although this won't be fully developed until chapters 9 and 10, keep your observational antennae out to pick up signals.

Keep in mind how these seven different groups respond to Jesus in the Gospel of Mark—the crowds, the Pharisees or religious leaders, his family and friends, the disciples, divine and demonic voices, and outsiders, especially Gentiles.

The Content of 2:1—3:6

A helpful aid to Bible study is the use of some type of structural diagram which shows in visual form the content and main emphases of a given passage. The diagram at the top of the next page portrays the structure of this segment, with the paragraphs divided and titled as suggested in the study questions. Are your paragraphs and titles similar? Identical? Note that each title *describes* the content. It does not interpret. First comes description; later comes interpretation.

The first story, the first twelve verses, describes Jesus healing the paralytic man. It's the story of letting a man down through the roof. Jesus heals the man's paralysis, and then comes reaction to the healing. Hence the title for this paragraph: *"Jesus Heals a Paralytic."*

In the second paragraph, *Jesus Calls Levi;* then *Jesus*

PARAGRAPH DIAGRAM OF MARK 2:1—3:6

Jesus Heals a Paralytic	Jesus Associates with Outcasts	Dispute on Fasting

2:1	2:12	2:13	2:17	2:18	2:22

Disciples Pluck Grain	Jesus Heals Withered Hand

2:23	2:28	3:1	3:6

On the Sabbath

Associates with Tax Collectors and Sinners. By putting these two incidents together, I suggest an appropriate descriptive title to be, *Jesus Associates with Outcasts.* In the first paragraph, Jesus not only healed the paralytic but also forgave the sins of the paralytic, which triggered opposition from the scribes. Now in this paragraph, Jesus associates with the wrong kind of people, even calling one to be his disciple. It's startling to note that Jesus called Levi. Levi, a tax collector, was not well accepted by the common people.

The third unit in the segment, verses 18-22, we might entitle the *Dispute on Fasting.* The key question is, Why don't your disciples fast as do John's disciples and the Pharisees? Why don't your disciples follow the regular religious customs?

In the next paragraph, verses 23 through 28 (see the horizontal line), *Jesus' Disciples Pluck Grain on the Sabbath.* Did you notice? The disciples pluck grain *on the sabbath,* and this also causes problems with those who observe. Why do Jesus and his disciples break the most sacred law of Judaism—the sabbath—as interpreted by the Jews at that time?

Then in 3:1-6 we have a sequel to 2:23-28. Jesus heals the man with the withered hand, again a violation of the sabbath.

These five paragraphs are all of similar nature. That's

why we study this as one unit. We call this a unified segment, since all the paragraphs are bound together by a common theme or motif. What is that common theme?

First Jesus heals the paralytic man, and this arouses reaction from the religious leaders. Then Jesus associates with the outcasts, and this creates another storm of protest. Then comes the dispute on fasting followed by two sabbath violations. The common theme is clearly the opposition of the religious leaders to Jesus' ministry.

Probing Deeper

Let's look more carefully and find out how the text records the negative reaction. In verse 7, note that after Jesus says to the paralytic, "My son, your sins are forgiven," some of the scribes (the scribes were recognized as the interpreters of the law) question in their hearts both Jesus' action and word. They murmur among themselves, "Why does this man speak thus?. . . Who can forgive sins but God alone?"

Note that word "why." It occurs again in verse 16. After Jesus associated and ate with tax collectors and sinners, ". . . the scribes of the Pharisees, when they saw that he was eating with sinners and tax collectors, said to his disciples, 'Why does he eat with tax collectors and sinners?' " We see the same response of protest.

Actually the Greek text contains added intensity in the second question. In the first case (verse 7) the normal Greek word for why, *ti,* occurs. In verse 16 *hoti* occurs, meaning "wherefore-why." The pressure of opposition is mounting. The Pharisees are stewing in their minds, "We don't understand this man; why does he do those things that are not customary for religious leaders to do?"

And then in verse 18, following the question on fasting, they again ask, "Why do John's disciples and the disciples of the Pharisees fast, but your disciples do not fast?" Here another word is used for "why." It's translated "why" in the

RSV but in the Greek it's *dia ti,* "on account of-why." Each time the probing is more intense and determined.

Finally, in the next paragraph, things become even more intense because Jesus touches the most sensitive nerve of the Pharisees and the religious leaders. That nerve is the sabbath. They knew full well that the cultural conditioning was such that when Jesus or his disciples could be shown to break the sabbath, the crowds could be easily moved against him. What we find in verse 24 is *Ide, ti,* "look-why" is this man doing what is not lawful on the sabbath? The insinuation, "look at him," carries a trace of scorn. The evidence has mounted against him!

In the last paragraph, however, no "why" occurs, as in the first four. Rather, as the text says, they were watching so that they might accuse him (verse 2). The situation is set up. They are now ready to submit the evidence against him and, hopefully, eventually get rid of him. So soon in the Gospel of Mark!

Two points deserve notice. First, observe the contrast between the crowd's response in 2:12 and the Pharisees' response in 3:5, 6. Note this and other observations on the structural diagram at the end of the exposition of this chapter. Second, note that the Pharisees take counsel with the Herodians, a most unlikely coalition! But why—why did they get together? The Pharisees had set themselves against Jesus and they recognized that the Herodians, a pro-Roman group with political leverage, might be able to give them the necessary aid and provide the connections to successfully plot Jesus' demise.

This odd company disappears from Mark's story until a more opportune time when they're finally ready with noose in hand! Look in 12:13; the question they raise hits a nerve as sensitive for the Jews *and* Romans as was the sabbath for the Jews! We shall return to it later.

Little wonder that the Gospel of Mark has been called

"a passion narrative with an extended introduction" (see note 2, ch. 10, p. 221. So, early in the Gospel Jesus faces the fate of his death. Already Jesus is a hunted man. His life is at stake!

Jesus' Counter-Response

1. In each of these conflict-incidents, Jesus answers the "why" questions with action and authority that send the interrogators reeling. In the first case his response is twofold: (1) by using the popular logic that sickness is the result of sin (which Jesus himself refuses in John 9), he demonstrates on their terms, through the evidence of the paralytic, the validity of his pronouncement, "My son, your sins are forgiven," and (2) he identifies himself with "the Son of man," the One who comes "with the clouds of heaven" and receives "dominion and glory and kingdom" from "all peoples, nations, and languages" (Daniel 7:13, 14).

The scribes' response? Shocked and angered to silence!

The crowds response? *Amazement*—a unique thing in all of history!

Actually, Jesus' forgiveness of sins was rank blasphemy, according to Jewish thought. Only God forgives sins and no man can play God! This was good Jewish theology—and sorely needed by many of us moderns! The failure of these scribes to accept Jesus' unique claim to forgive sins, however, became their fatal flaw, for Jesus was no ordinary person. Rather than concluding that the situation did not fit the rules, they should have perceived that their rules did not fit the situation.

True, such a lunatic claim could normally be discounted. It would come to naught without anyone taking action against it. But the healed man continued to provide both visual and verbal evidence against them. The second level of the response was no less incisive. In Daniel the "Son of man" was a figure of ultimate, transcendent regal power. For Jesus to identify himself thus was too much for normal thought structures. Who, anyway, is this one who claims ultimate authority (*exousia*) upon earth?

2. In the second conflict-encounter Jesus also confounds the conventions of scribal piety: "Those who are well have no need of a physician, but those who are sick; I came not to call the righteous, but sinners" (verse 17).

He who has supreme authority, one would think, would call kings and religious leaders into his cabinet and prepare to run the world right. But not so Jesus. He called the despised, the outcasts, those who come not in majesty but brokenness—broken by the oppression and indifference of the powerful, broken by the very ones expecting to rule with "the coming king"!

3. Jesus' answer in the third round is more complex. It contains three sets of images: wedding guests and a bridegroom, an unshrunk patch and an old garment, new wine and old wineskins. Together, these images answer the question as to why his disciples don't fast.

The first set of images is a cryptic announcement, for those who have ears to hear it. When there are wedding guests and a bridegroom, there is indeed a wedding. What's going on? Apparently the questioners of Jesus aren't up with the times. They don't know that a wedding is going on right in their midst: "The time is fulfilled, and the kingdom of God is at hand . . ." (1:15). No time to fast; time to celebrate! The wedding banquet is on! Jesus, for God's sake, is calling a new bride and hence the new age is dawning (compare Hosea 2:14-23; Jeremiah 31:31-34)!

Further, the power of this new reality cannot be contained by the old religion and tradition. It's like an unshrunk patch sewn onto an old garment or new wine stored in old brittle skins. The two won't go together. The old rites of Judaism cannot contain the new power of the kingdom which Jesus is bringing. New wine needs new skins. And already Jesus' followers, though few, are a new bunch; they're not fasting according to custom.

4. Jesus' replies to his accusers over his sabbath conduct cut through all the Pharisees' picky rules for the sabbath and rescue for all time this blessed institution from its pharisaic captivity. Jesus eases into his explosive manifesto by recounting an occasion when David broke the rules for the sake of human need (verses 25-27). Then the explosion: "The sabbath was made for man, not man for the sabbath; so the Son of man [that title again] is Lord even of the sabbath." Jesus claims authority (*exousia*) or lordship even over the sabbath, the most sacred institution of Judaism.

What really was the original purpose of the sabbath anyway? Rest? Yes, but for what purpose? To do nothing? "Is it lawful on the sabbath to do good or to do harm, to save life or to kill?" Jesus' question faces us with the *moral* purpose of the sabbath, an emphasis long forgotten by legalistic developments within Judaism. Is not rest related to health, life, and the whole community's well-being?

One of the earliest Old Testament texts on the sabbath zeros in on the moral purposes of the sabbath. In Deuteronomy 5:12-15 the sabbath is given (1) so "that your manservant and your maidservant may rest as well as you" and (2) as a time to celebrate deliverance from slavery in Egypt (when they didn't ever have any rest!). The sabbath stands for salvation and equal privilege in the community. It is actually a humanitarian institution, affirming God's grace of redemption and the social justice which that grace proclaims for life in this world.

No wonder that the *sabbath*-sabbatical system means freeing the slaves, canceling debts, and, on every fiftieth year, redistributing the land! "The sabbath was made for man, not man for the sabbath!" And no wonder that Jesus, who fulfills the humanitarian vision of the sabbath says, "Come to me, all who labor and are heavy laden, and I will give you rest" (Matthew 11:28). Amazingly, this is the preface to these two

sabbath stories in Matthew's Gospel (12:1-14). No wonder
that Jesus claims lordship over the sabbath. He knew what
God intended through the sabbath and Jesus' deeds were
making good those intentions.

Questions from the religious type and Jesus' answers—
an encounter of history! Never again will religion be secure in
its easy legalisms, pieties, and platitudes. The man of Galilee,
the "Son of man," confronts us with a call to the kingdom
which secure religion cannot comprehend, contain, nor overcome.

> O Lord,
>   What has happened to your people?
>   those, whom you called,
>   those, to whom you gave
>   the law, the priests, and the prophets!
>   How and why did it happen—
>   that law became rules,
>   knowledge became categories, and
>   faith became religion?
>   Save us from our own pharisaic selves—
>   lest our theology stifle your forgiveness,
>   our conventions ostracize the outcasts, and
>   our legalisms fight your liberation.
>   Awaken us,
>   to see you
>   as you truly are—
>   Lord!
>   Amen.

STRUCTURAL DIAGRAM OF MARK 2:1—3:6

THE CONFLICT STORIES

Jesus Heals a Paralytic	Jesus Associates with Outcasts	Question on Fasting	Jesus' Disciples Pluck Grain	Jesus Heals Withered Hand
2:1 2:12	2:13 2:17	2:18 2:22	2:23 2:28	3:1 3:6

On the Sabbath

Responses to Jesus

Crowds Amazed (12)

Contrast

Pharisees and Herodians Seek to Kill Jesus (6)

Scribes	Scribes of Pharisees	Disciples of John and Pharisees	Pharisees	Pharisees
Why? (v. 7)	Why? (v. 16)	Why? (v. 18)	Look, Why? (v.24)	Watching to Accuse (v. 2)
Ti (Τί)	Hoti ("Οτι)	Dia ti (Διὰ τί)	Ide ti ("Ιδε τί)	

Jesus' Replies

2:10 ——— 2:17 ——— 2:19-22 ——— 2:27,28 ——— 3:4

Reflection, Discussion, and Action

1. How did we move so quickly into such a tense situation between Jesus and the religious leaders? True, we skipped chapter 1 (we will come back to it), but even so Jesus is deep into conflict almost at the outset. Read Luke 4:16-30 and notice the same point in Luke after Jesus' sermon at Nazareth.

2. You probably wonder why I started with chapter 2 instead of 1. Mostly because chapter 1, especially the introduction in verses 1-15, can be better understood after one sees the emphases of the larger Gospel. We'll pick up 1:21-45 in lesson five. Also, it is easier for a beginner in the inductive method to discover the unifying theme(s) of 2:1—3:6 than it is to see them in 1:21-45. So we have eased into the study by focusing on a segment where correct observations are more easily perceived.

3. Now since you've read the exposition and studied the structural diagram, do you think you correctly checked question eight in your presession study? I would check a, c, and d "yes." Throughout the segment the same *persons,* Jesus and the Pharisees, are on center stage. The *events* are presented as events of conflict which in turn function as the unifying *idea* or concept of the segment. We don't know when each event occurred (time) nor do we know the specific places. These were not important to Mark and are therefore not stressed.

4. Who in this segment (2:1—3:6) most closely matches your attitudes when long-held traditions are threatened: the crowds (amazed), the Pharisees (hostile), or the disciples (sympathetic, but uncommitted)? Read Mark 7:1-23 for more information on this problem.

5. To what aspects in your life or your congregation's life does Jesus' teaching on "old wineskins" speak? What evidences of "new wine" have there been in your life or in your congregation this past year?

6. How do we test whether new challenges are the "new

wine" from Jesus or the "pressures of the world" seeking to conform us to its values?

7. Since we are to be *followers* of Jesus, how does faithfulness to his deeds and teachings relate to change itself? Might the "new wine" for us mean the recovery of the old? What kind of values are characteristic of the wine of Jesus? See Jesus' five responses in this segment.

Chapter 3

Jesus Speaks in Parables:
The Disciples' Responsibility

(Mark 4:1-34)

Presession Study

1. Notice that we omitted 3:7-35 for the moment. Verses 7-12 are an extended summary and this chapter will refer to verses 13-19. But we will return later to observe the meaning of these verses in the Gospel.

2. Read 4:1-34, draw a horizontal line and provide space on it for each paragraph. Give each paragraph a descriptive title.

3. What specific feature sets these verses off as a separate segment distinct from the preceding and following paragraphs?

4. Do these paragraphs have one central emphasis or several? How do the keynote verses in Mark 1:14, 15 relate to this passage? In each case Jesus is proclaiming and teaching about _____.

5. What is the meaning of verses 11, 12? Why did Jesus use parables? How do these verses relate to verses 21-25?

6. Read the entire Gospel of Mark, in one sitting if

possible. One writer calls the Gospel *Mysterious Revelation.* Why?

7. What emphasis do all these parables share in common? What do they teach about the kingdom of God?

EXPOSITION: MARK 4:1-34

In this chapter we focus on Mark 4:1-34. This segment contains four or five of Jesus' parables. Except for parabolic riddles in 3:23 ff. and the allegorical parable in 12:1-9, these are the only parables of Jesus recorded by Mark. Both Matthew and Luke record many, many more parables, but John's Gospel records none. All together the Synoptic Gospels (Matthew, Mark, and Luke)[1] record approximately thirty-five parables of Jesus.

Since Mark selects only a few of Jesus' parables, we rightly might expect that he emphasizes also selected, distinctive themes in his chosen parables. Our study will verify this expectation.

The first nine verses of 4:1-34 tell the *Parable of the Sower.* Verses 10-12 might be viewed as a separate paragraph, although the RSV does not show them as such. These verses, perhaps the most difficult in the New Testament to understand, I'll entitle *Reason for Parables.* They read: "To you has been given the secret of the kingdom of God, but for those outside everything is in parables; so that they may indeed see but not perceive, and may indeed hear but not understand; lest they should turn again, and be forgiven."

It sounds as though Jesus spoke in parables in order that people wouldn't catch on because, if they would, they might repent and become converted. This goes against the grain of everything our preachers, Sunday school teachers, mothers, and fathers ever taught us about the gospel. Did Jesus use parables to deliberately obscure the message from the multitudes? That's what it says, but is such possible? We'll come back to this later; then I'll make a few suggestions for understanding this difficult teaching.

Verses 13-20 consist of the *Interpretation of the Parable of the Sower,* a fairly familiar story. In verses 21-25, we have two mini-parables, the *Parable of the Lamp* and the *Parable of the Measure.* Verse 24 says: "Take heed what you hear; the measure you give will be the measure you get, and still more will be given you. For to him who has will more be given; and from him who has not, even what he has will be taken away." That's also a rather difficult saying to understand. We'll come back to it as well.

The next not-so-familiar but very interesting parable in verses 26-29 occurs only in Mark's Gospel, a rare phenomenon. Almost everything that occurs in Mark occurs also in Matthew and Luke; but this parable appears only in Mark. I entitle it, *The Parable of the Seed Growing Secretly.* The seed grows while the farmer merely sleeps and rises. Suddenly, without announcement or fanfare, the seed sprouts and grows. The blade appears, then the ear, then the full grain on the ear, and finally comes harvest—mysterious growth and certain harvest, just like the kingdom of God.

The next parable in verses 30-32 is quite well known, the *Parable of the Mustard Seed.* The mustard seed is so tiny, but it grows and produces a tree so large that even the birds of the air come and make their nests in its branches.

So here we have four parables: the sower parable, followed later by the interpretation; the lamp and measure parables (by putting these together as one parable we get a total of four); then the parable of the seed growing secretly; and finally the parable of the mustard seed. These four parables are grouped together here in this section of Mark's Gospel.

Key Terms and Leading Themes

What are the leading themes and key terms in this particular segment?

1. First of all, we should notice what is obvious. This is a segment on the *Parables.* These are the parables of Jesus. The word itself is used first in this segment in verse 2: "And he taught them many things in parables, and in his teaching he

said to them: 'Listen! A sower went out to sow.' " The word
parable occurs again in verse 10, where it says that a smaller
group, primarily the twelve, asked Jesus privately about the
parables. Then in verse 13 Jesus says: "Do you not understand this parable? How then will you understand all the
parables?" Finally, in verses 33 and 34: "With many such
parables he spoke the word to them, as they were able to hear
it; he did not speak to them without a parable, but privately
to his own disciples he explained everything." That's the first
observation we make. This is the segment on the parables of
Jesus.

Parables about what? The word *parabole* means to "cast
alongside." Literally, that's the meaning. It's putting a story
alongside a truth, or clothing the truth with a story. I am sure
you've heard this definition of the word parable: "an earthly
story with a heavenly meaning." I remember that from my
early, probably intermediate Sunday school years, and it has
stuck with me. In a way it's true, but it doesn't say everything.
If we take the word "heavenly" in the sense of kingdom
reality, then I think it's true. The only problem is that it might
leave the impression that this kingdom reality is always a
heavenly future reality. But through Jesus and his community, the kingdom manifests itself upon earth, in space and
time, here and now. Jesus came and announced that the
kingdom is here in our midst. Remember that point: if it's a
"heavenly meaning"—it's a kingdom reality that is not
removed to another realm of life, but a kingdom truth that
addresses us here and now about responsibilities and op-
portunities in this life.

2. For a second major theme, look in verse 11: "To you
has been given the secret of the kingdom of God." Jesus is
teaching the disciples about the *kingdom of God*. Also verse
26: "And he said, 'The kingdom of God is as if a man should
scatter seed upon the ground,' " and, again in verse 30: "With
what can we compare the kingdom of God?" This segment is

obviously devoted to the parables of the kingdom of God.

What do we learn about the kingdom from these parables? What do they tell us about the nature of the kingdom?
Did you notice that all of these parables portray a small beginning but envision also a big, surprise harvest at the end?
Even the little grain of mustard seed grows into a big tree.
The grain that falls into the ground while the farmer sleeps
grows secretly, then bursts forth, and finally makes a harvest.
Or, you don't put a lamp under a bushel. Whatever is hid is
hid in order to become manifest. You don't have a secret—
except that it one day will be told! As children we had secrets
which we tried to keep from certain people. Secrets are to
keep, but the keeping is only temporary. We will tell them
sometime. This is an analogy for the kingdom.

Something quite significant, though secretive, is happening in and through the life of Jesus. One day it's going to become manifest for all to see. But now it's shrouded in secrecy,
even in the parable of the sower. It is true that the parable of
the sower says that some seed fell by the way and was lost,
some seed fell on the rock and didn't bring forth fruit, and
some seed was choked out by the thorns.

But do you know where the punch line of the parable is?
Despite all the opposition, some seed does fall on good
ground and it bears fruit—thirtyfold, sixtyfold, and a hundredfold! That's the punch line of the parable. Despite all the
opposition, the growth of the kingdom is certain, even
though it has small beginnings. The people as a whole did not
recognize what was going on. Certainly the Pharisees had no
idea what was happening in their midst. At least they
wouldn't admit it. But something was going on, and it would
one day catch up people from all over the world including
you, your study group, your congregation, your denomination, and Christians from all nations of the globe. The seed of
the word has taken root in us and we are part of the growth of
that kingdom.

3. Note several other important themes in this text. I already alluded to one—the mention of the secret. "To you has been given the secret of the kingdom." (The King James Version says, "the mystery of the kingdom.") Look also in verse 22: "For there is nothing hid, except to be made manifest; nor is anything secret, except to come to light." The secrecy theme is very tantalizing in the Gospel. In 26 and 27, while the man is sleeping, the seed is growing, and it is secretive growth. It's going on while people do not notice.

4. But now having said all this, we have not yet identified the central theme of this segment. There is one word that occurs, one, two, three, four, five, six, seven, eight, nine, ten, eleven times. Did you notice it? Can you discover it for yourself? In the midst of the teaching of the parables, there is an injunction, an imperative, an exhortation. Do you know what it is? Maybe it's hard to pick up in some versions because the word is sometimes translated differently. But it's always the same word in the Greek text. It's the word "hear," "listen," "pay attention" (in Greek *akouo*). When the parables are spoken, we stand before judgment. Are we listening, hearing, and understanding? Our response is crucial.

Turn now to the structural diagram at the end of this exposition and note the recurring use of the term "hear," as well as the other observations made thus far. In 4:3 the RSV text translates it "listen." Some translations have the word "hear." "Hear! A sower went out to sow." Both verses 9 and 23 contain the exhortation: "He who has ears to hear, let him hear." In verse 12 it occurs in the quotation, "so that they may indeed . . . hear but not understand." In verses 14-20 it occurs four times: the four soils are compared to the kinds of "hearing" in the people (verses 15, 16, 18, 20). Verse 24 then says, "Take heed what you hear; the measure you give will be the measure you get, and still more will be given you."

Please, please don't apply these two verses to economics. That is wrenching statements out of context. It may be true that the rich get richer and the poor get poorer, but let's not use or misuse the Bible to support social evil and make the Bible justify bad social conditions in the world. That is both bad exegesis and unchristian ethics.

This text is about *hearing,* about paying attention. The extent that you genuinely hear will determine how much you understand from the teachings of Jesus. "For to the one who has will more be given." When someone hears or listens, insight will grow and understanding will grow. But from the one who "has not," or hears nothing (and I think here of the Pharisees who didn't seem to open up their minds one little crack to what Jesus had to say), even the opportunity to hear will be taken away.

Note that in 3:6, 7 Jesus went out of the synagogue and after that taught by the seaside, on the mountain, or on the way to Jerusalem, but not again in the synagogue to the Pharisees (with the exception of his visit to his home town in 6:1-6). Finally in verse 33, it says: "With many such parables he spoke the word to them, as they were able to hear it." Hence the predominant emphasis of this segment is on hearing and understanding. To the one who gets some understanding more will be given. That's the crucial issue in this segment on the parables.

5. Notice yet another point: the segment begins in verse 1 with Jesus addressing a great multitude, but then in verses 10-12 ff. his teaching is addressed to the *disciples.* They have been called to be with Jesus (3:13-19) and to learn more intensely the meaning of the kingdom. Who are the disciples now following Jesus, according to the record? In 1:16-20 Jesus called four disciples to follow him—Peter and Andrew, James and John—by the Sea of Galilee. In 2:13 he called Levi, probably to be identified with Matthew (see Matthew 9:9). Then in 3:13-19 Jesus "went up on the mountain, and called to him those whom he desired." On the mountain "he made twelve" (as the Greek text says), or, as the RSV puts it,

"he appointed twelve." The verb could be translated "create"; Jesus *created* the twelve. A significant number of manuscripts repeat the phrase in verse 16, "and he made the twelve."[2]

In chapter 4 then, Jesus preaches about the kingdom and explains "the secret of the kingdom" to his disciples. Does the act of constituting twelve on the mountain ring any memory-bells of previous similar acts? Look in Exodus 24 and discover that Moses also constituted the twelve tribes of Israel on a mountain. As Paul Minear indicates in his commentary on Mark, Jesus intentionally chose "twelve" in order to form a new Israel.[3] The kingdom of God is proclaimed as God's special gift to this newly formed community, founded by Jesus.

Why the Secret (4:11, 12)?

Now we must look more closely at the meaning of the "secret" and investigate those puzzling verses addressed primarily to the twelve: "To you has been given the secret of the kingdom of God, but for those outside everything is in parables; so that they may indeed see but not perceive, they may indeed hear but not understand; lest they should turn again, and be forgiven." This is a very puzzling, difficult text! Did Jesus use parables in order to keep people from understanding, repenting, and joining the kingdom?

Various explanations of the difficulty have been given. *The Living Bible,* for example, tries to cover the difficulty by making the people responsible for their refusal to hear. But that approach ignores what the text says. The solution must be found along other lines. I'll offer three suggestions that may be helpful, with the third one, in my judgment, being the most helpful.

1. One scholar, Joachim Jeremias, resolves the difficulty by showing that these two verses, quoted from Isaiah 6:9, 10, are dependent not upon the Hebrew Old Testament text, nor

the Greek (Septuagint) translation(s) of Isaiah, but upon one of the Aramaic translations, known as the Targums. The Aramaic term (*dilema*) in the Targum, the word behind the English "lest" in 12c, has three different meanings. Its first two meanings (1) "in order that not" and (2) "lest perhaps" are also possible translations of the Greek word used in Mark's text (*mepote*). But the Aramaic *dilema* has also a third meaning, "unless."[4]

By allowing this meaning, "unless," the problem disappears. Let's read the text with this translation: "To you has been given the secret of the kingdom of God, but for those outside everything is in parables; so that they may indeed see but not perceive, and may indeed hear but not understand; *unless* they should turn again, and be forgiven." Then, of course, if they repent, they would understand. The difficulty is solved with one bold brilliant stroke.

But the problem remains, for that is not what the biblical text says. The solution is an explanation of its meaning in Aramaic, but all the earliest manuscripts for the New Testament were written not in Aramaic, but in Greek. So we're still left with the question, What did Mark, led by the inspiration of God, intend this text to mean? We have to deal with the text as it is and seek to understand Mark's intended meaning.

2. The second explanation, or better, consideration, that has been given is that we should remember that the Hebrew language and mind (the Old Testament background) did not distinguish between "result" and "purpose," apparently because of the Hebraic faith's high view of the sovereignty of God. What turns out as "result" is also understood to be divine purpose. In this case, Mark (writing around AD 65) had already witnessed the result of various people's response to Jesus' claims. Since many Jews refused to believe the messianic claims, this *result* is also regarded as *purpose*. I consider this somewhat helpful. The case of Pharaoh's hardened heart in Exodus serves as a parallel. Some texts say

Pharaoh hardened his own heart; others say God hardened his heart. The result (Pharaoh hardened his heart) is also regarded as divine purpose (God hardened his heart).

3. The third consideration builds on this point and provides a wider frame of reference. This particular verse is a quotation from Isaiah 6:9 where it describes the hardness of the hearts of the people. In the New Testament this verse is used at a number of other very crucial places also to explain why many Jews refused to accept Jesus as Messiah.

The quotation is used at the end of Acts (28:25-28) to explain the Jewish failure to understand the gospel and the subsequent Gentile acceptance of the gospel. It is used in John 12:39, 40 to explain again why the Jews failed to understand and accept Jesus as Messiah. It's used in the same chapter where some *Greeks* come to Philip and inquire about Jesus, after which Jesus declares that the hour of his glorification has now come! So in John as well, it functions as an explanation of why the gospel was refused by the Jews but accepted by the Gentiles. It is also alluded to in Romans 11:8, in that very difficult section of Romans 9-11, where Paul discusses the mystery of the gospel for both the Jews and the Gentiles. Finally, both Matthew (13:14, 15) and Luke (8:10) use the quotation, but in softened form, indicating that parables are appropriate for those disposed to unbelief.

It appears, therefore, that Mark is using this text to explain the difficult developments in salvation-history—that many, even most Jews refused to accept Jesus' messianic kingdom. This result is viewed thus also as the divine purpose, which occasioned the turning toward and including of the Gentiles. "Those outside," in verse 11, refers most likely to the mass of the Jewish crowds; but to those few, the Twelve, is given the secret of the kingdom, for they are to be the bearers of the new kingdom reality unto all nations, to the Gentiles, who upon hearing the word bring forth fruit, some thirtyfold, some sixtyfold, and some a hundredfold.[5]

But even the disciples don't understand (verse 13), at least not without explanation. Mark's Gospel dramatizes the disciples' struggle to understand who Jesus is. It is extremely difficult for them to comprehend Jesus. "To *you* is given the *secret* of the kingdom," but they still don't catch on. Why not?

Secrecy is at the heart of the Gospel's drama. After the first verse which identifies Jesus as "Son of God,"[6] Jesus' identity remains a secret. When Jesus does mighty works, he clearly commands those present not to tell anyone. Don't tell anyone, hush up, hush up! Look in 1:24, 25. Immediately Jesus hushes up the unclean spirit in the synagogue. In 1:34, after a mass healing at sundown, Jesus commands that no one be told; he does not permit the demons to speak. In 1:44 after the healing of the leper, Jesus strictly warns the leper, "Don't tell anyone!" (Now maybe I should use that technique also. You can read this book but don't tell anyone what you learned. What would be your response?)

Sometimes when students wrestle with this feature of Mark's Gospel they come up with the idea that this is good psychology. If you tell people not to tell, they will be sure to tell anyway. But I don't think that's the answer. The answer is more deeply embedded in the nature of Jesus' ministry and the different responses to it.

In 3:11 Mark clearly states that the demons wanted to announce who Jesus was and Jesus would not allow them to speak. He hushed up the demons. In 5:43, after Jesus healed Jarius' daughter, he clearly commanded that no one be told. In 7:36 after the healing of a deaf mute, Jesus "charged them to tell no one." In 8:30, after Peter confesses Jesus to be the Messiah, again we have his "hush up, don't tell anyone" instructions. In 9:9 we have a hint—just a hint—as to how we might explain the secrecy theme. As Jesus and the "inner three" were coming down from the mountain of transfiguration, Jesus commanded them not to tell anyone until after he had risen from the dead. It appears as though the truth about this person, Jesus, could not be fully or truly understood until after his death and resurrection.

Imagine yourself in the disciples' shoes! How would you know who Jesus is? The disciples, good nationalistic Jews, would have had a wrong view of messiahship. Hence, the secret! Even after Peter confessed Jesus as Messiah (8:29), he didn't understand his own confession on Jesus' terms. In 8:31-33, Peter's wrong view of messiahship is shockingly clear. But long before Peter said anything, the demons cried out, "O Holy one of God" (1:24), "You are the Son of God" (3:11; 5:7). But then always, "Hush up, hush up!" Not only do we hear the demonic cries in the Gospel, but two very important voices come from above—the divine voices.

At the baptism a voice proclaimed, "You are my beloved Son (Psalm 2:7), in whom I am well pleased" (Isaiah 42:1),[7] a statement of kingship (from Psalm 2:7) and servanthood (from Isaiah 42:1).

In Mark 9:7, on the mount of transfiguration, a voice said, "This is my beloved Son (again Psalm 2:7); listen to him" (from Deuteronomy 18:15, denoting the prophetic role).

Here are the voices. The demons are hushed up! But the voices from heaven are not hushed! The disciples, however, do not know who Jesus is. And they're slow to catch on.[8]

To understand this, put yourself back in the disciples place. It's hard for you to appreciate their situation because you've likely been told who Jesus is many times over. You know the answer, but you've forgotten the question: *Who is Jesus?* Identify with those disciples first called to follow Jesus and try to comprehend with them who this man, Jesus, is—speaking in riddles, doing mighty works, and running into conflict with the Pharisees. Who is he anyway?

In the drama of this Gospel, *heaven* knows and *hell* knows, but *humans* do not know. The divine voices and the

demonic voices tell the reader, but the disciples are struggling, struggling, and struggling to understand. In this way
Mark writes his Gospel to help his first readers and us come
to grips with the fundamental question, Who is this man,
Jesus? And even though we know the answer, do we know its
meaning?!

O Lord Jesus,
we too are your disciples
who should know
but don't understand.
Some of us have studied much
and others less,
some have forsaken much
and others less;
but we still need explanations
and our following falters.
Perhaps it's because we mix up
the important and the routine;
We see You, Jesus, as just another rabbi,
an outstanding teacher,
and even a miracle-worker.
But we are not ready for encounter
with the Son of man
the transcendent Lord
of glory
and cross.
We're listening to the kingdom teaching.
Help us HEAR
and UNDERSTAND.
Amen.

STRUCTURAL DIAGRAM OF MARK 4:1-34

THE PARABLES

"The Sower"		Reason for Parables	Interpretation of the "Sower"	Lamp and Measure	Seed Growing Secretly	Mustard Seed	Use of Parables
4:1	4:9	4:10 4:12	4:13 4:20	4:21 4:25	4:26 4:29	4:30 4:32	4:33 4:34

Key Themes in the Segment

parables
v.2 ————— v.10 ————— v.13 ————————————————————— vv.33, 34

"the kingdom of God"
v.11 ————————————— v.26 ————— v.30

"secret"-secrecy
v.11 ————————— v.22 ————— (v.27)

"hear and understand"
v.3 ——— v.9 ——— vv. 12,13 ——— 15, 16, 18, 20 ——— 23, 24 ——————————— v.33

Reflection, Discussion, and Action

1. These parables emphasize the certainty of the kingdom's growth, despite opposition, and a bountiful harvest at the end. Is this how you feel about the church and the missionary cause of the gospel? What kind of mood and outlook should this generate in us as witnesses for the kingdom of God?

2. Image how a first-century Christian preacher would apply verses 14-20 of this segment to his congregation, especially during times of persecution. When the parable of the sower was used then or is used now, where should we put the emphasis? On the rocks and the thorns? Or on the fruit and harvest?

3. F. F. Bruce has written a book entitled *The Spreading Flame.* What emphases in this segment suggest such a title in describing the expansion of Christianity? To what event does verse 29 refer? What do we mean by the term "kingdom of God"?

4. If you are studying in a group, give time for each member to share signs of kingdom growth within the congregation, conference, or larger church, including home and overseas missions. (*As group leader, you may wish to make assignments on this.*)

5. What influences are keeping us as Christians from hearing, understanding, and obeying the gospel? Think of your own congregation and denomination. Where are the "hearing" problems?

6. How does the emphasis of this study fit with that of the last chapter? What is the relationship between accepting "new wine" and "faithful hearing" which includes obedience?

7. Pledge to yourself that, given the next opportunity, you will witness for the kingdom of God, telling someone the gospel news, that Jesus is ___.

Just Like That

CHORIC

Just like that
Jesus of Nazareth
                walks out of the desert
                into Galilee
                and announces:
it's here
the kingdom of God
is here!
                like he had brought it
                with him—
                        as if he himself
                        embodied
                        the kingdom—
                                        he said
you must change
                your hearts
                and minds
                and believe the good news:
it's here
the kingdom of God
is here;
                                you must change
                                your hearts
                                and minds
                which are convinced
                the kingdom
                was or will be;
                                        you
                                        must
                                        change
                                        and

stop living in a noble history
where the only reality is
the past tense;

> you
> must
> change
> and

stop living in the futile speculation
about a future
which is fully in the hand of God—
a future
which is always beyond now—
a future which
can never be
a present reality—
or if it is...
(a present reality)
...is not future!

> you
> must
> change
> and

believe the good news—
it's here
the kingdom of God
is here

> *Now*

believe the good news
God's kingdom is here

That seems to be the message:
the kingdom
came in
with Jesus,
the kingdom
is
where Jesus is;
you must change
your hearts
and minds
and believe the good news.

who is this man
who
walks out of the desert
into Galilee
and announces—
it's here
the kingdom of God
is here

—From *To Walk in the Way*

Chapter 4

Jesus Does Mighty Works: The Disciples' Question

(Mark 4:35—6:6)

Presession Study

1. The Gospel of Mark is known as "the Gospel of Action." It is often noted that Mark's Gospel, in comparison to the other Gospels, contains a higher percentage of the deeds of Jesus and a lower percentage of the words of Jesus. That may seem difficult to understand at the moment because the last chapter concentrated on the words of Jesus, the parables. But if we compare Mark 4 with Matthew 13 we notice that Matthew has many more parables than Mark does. Likewise, if we compare Mark with Luke we find that Luke has a "special section," 9:51 through 19:27, most of which consists of teaching, with many parables, and most of which is not found in Mark.

So Mark is known as the Gospel of action, the Gospel of Jesus' deeds. I suggest that this contributes to the dramatic nature of the Gospel. Further it contributes to the mood of urgency, denoted also by the frequently recurring term, *euthus,* translated "immediately" or "straightforward." In rapid fire succession, Mark portrays one event happening immediately after another.

Read quickly Mark 1:1—4:34 and notice how often Mark uses the word "immediately" (the KJV translation is "straightway").

2. Read Mark 4:35—6:6. In the sequence of our studies this is now a third segment of similar stories from the life of Jesus. What does such combining of similar stories and teachings tell us about the origin, nature, and purpose of this Gospel? Do you think these incidents all happened at the same time? If so, when? Or does the Gospel present thematic groupings of events that happened over a period of time?

3. Portray the separate paragraphs on a horizontal line chart and give each one a descriptive title. Compare this segment with Luke 8:22-56 and Matthew 8:23—9:26. What is different about Matthew?

4. Does Mark use any key terms which tell us what types of stories he selected for this segment? Read 6:1-6 carefully. Did you find the answer?

5. What thematic emphases emerge in this segment? Are there any repeated words or phrases? Portray the occurrence of these on your horizontal line diagram.

6. Reflect upon the nature of these four events. What is the significance of each event? What do these mighty deeds tell us about Jesus? How do you explain 5:43? What about 5:19?!

7. As we compare these three snapshots of Jesus' ministry (2:1—3:6; 4:1-34; and now 4:35—6:6), what kind of portrait of the man, Jesus, emerges? How does this compare with popular images of Jesus?

EXPOSITION: MARK 4:35–6:6

In this chapter we'll look at what are called "the mighty works" of Jesus, "the mighty wonders" or "miracles." It's interesting to note that similar types of events are placed together in the Gospel: the miracles are together, the parables are together, and the conflict stories are together in units which we've called segments. When I see that, I raise the question: how did Mark organize the events and teachings of Jesus? Do we have a chronological account in the book of Mark, yes or no? How are the stories of Jesus organized?

It appears that we have what might be called sermonic groupings. Similar events are brought together in one place. These may have been used as sermons in the church, preached perhaps by Peter himself, since the early church fathers unanimously recognize Mark's dependence upon Peter. When we look at quotations from the early church fathers we discover that this indeed is how they understood the Gospel of Mark. The fourth-century historian, Eusebius, quotes Papias from the second century:

> And the Elder [John] said this also. Mark, having become the interpreter of Peter, wrote down accurately all that he remembered of the things said and done by the Lord, but not however in order. For neither did he hear the Lord, nor did he follow Him, but afterwards, as I said, Peter, who adapted his teachings to the needs (of the hearers), but not as though he were drawing up a connected account of the Lord's oracles. So then Mark made no mistake in thus recording some things just as he remembered them, for he made it his one care to omit nothing that he had heard and to make no false statement therein.[1]

This quotation, along with others in Appendix I, indicates that Mark did not write the events of Jesus in chronological order, but rather in thematic groupings. As I read these segments with common emphases, I can imagine

Peter himself preaching, stressing in one sermon Jesus' conflict with Jewish leaders; in another, the parables of Jesus; and in still another, Jesus' mighty deeds.

The Content of the Segment
In this segment we observe a series of deeds which shows Jesus' power over all obstacles that resist his presence and power. In 4:35-41 *Jesus Stills the Storm;* in the second story, 5:1-20, *Jesus Heals the Gerasene Demoniac.* The third paragraph, though it begins at 5:21, is not completed until verse 43 since another story is sandwiched into the middle of it. This sandwiching of one story into another is an interesting Markan technique which Mark uses several times elsewhere, as we will see later. Mark begins one story; then suddenly another story begins in the middle of the first one. So in 5:24b-34 *Jesus Heals the Woman with a Hemorrhage* and then Mark finishes the story he began in verse 21, in which *Jesus Raises Jairus' Daughter.* So here we have two incidents of healing, or, better, a healing and a resurrection; and these two are intertwined with each other, sandwiched together.

I've also included 6:1-6 in this segment. You may wonder why. These verses are known as *Jesus' Rejection at Nazareth.* Read these verses to see if you can discover the connection. While no mighty work is narrated in these verses, nonetheless, they do refer back to the mighty works that were just recorded. Look in verse 2: "Where did this man get all this?" He comes to his hometown, Nazareth, and his home people want to know where he got all this! "What is the wisdom given to him? What *mighty works* are wrought by his hands!" *(italics mine).*

In the text itself we have the clue that tells us what we have been reading about from 4:35 onward—"the mighty works of Jesus." The account says, "They took offense at him. And Jesus said to them, 'A prophet is not without honor, except in his own country, and among his own kin, and in his own house.' And he could do no *mighty work* there, except that he laid his hands upon a few sick people and healed them. And he marveled because of their unbelief." (italics mine). There's where this segment ends: "He marveled because of their unbelief." This point contrasts sharply with the emphasis on *faith* enunciated earlier in the segment.

Secrecy, But . . . .
     Characteristic of Mark, in 5:43 the raising of Jairus' daughter is not to be told. But in 5:19 we hear a rather uncharacteristic remark! The demoniac, healed and sane, wants to follow Jesus but Jesus tells him to go home and tell everyone what has happened. That's amazing! It's a change of style, totally out of keeping with what we see everywhere else in Mark's Gospel. Elsewhere Jesus says, "Be quiet, be quiet, hush up, hush up, don't tell, don't tell." But in this case he instructs the man, "Go home and tell everybody!"
     Can you figure out why this exception occurs? Perhaps a hint will help. Note the location of this event. Might that make a difference? If you don't feel you have a final answer now, that's all right; the answer will come in the next chapters. But keep the question on your agenda: why the difference between 5:19 and 5:43?
     Look at the structural diagram of this segment to see how the emphases of this segment are summarized and portrayed.

Understanding Faith and Miracles
     Look back in 5:34 and 5:36. In verse 34 in the story of the woman with a hemorrhage Jesus said to her, "Daughter, your faith has made you well; go in peace, and be healed of your disease." And again in connection with Jairus' daughter, in verse 36, Jesus said to Jairus, "Do not fear, only believe." Jesus affirms and calls forth faith on the part of these persons. That accords with what we read in 4:40 in

the stilling of the storm. That incident also ends with the punch line, "Why are you afraid, disciples? Don't you have any faith?"

Hence, Mark emphasizes Jesus' call to faith in this segment. Though not present in the story of the Gerasene demoniac, the theme does occur in the other three incidents and especially in the healing of the woman with the flow of blood. But while the disciples are chided for lack of faith, his home people judged for unbelief, and the ruler of the synagogue called to faith, only the woman (note: a *woman*) is commended for her actual, expressed faith.

Two questions press upon us for answers: is faith a prerequisite for the unleashing of Jesus' power, and how do we understand 6:5, 6a? Certain faith healers today would have us think that all illness could be healed if only we would have enough faith. Is this idea biblical? Of the four events reported here, only one shows faith present in the connection with Jesus' effectual power. And even that faith is affirmed *after* the healing occurred. One might say, however, that of these incidents, only this one was a healing, the only one where faith would or could be expressed. The dead girl, the demoniac, and the sea couldn't express faith. While that reply is significant, the events in chapter 1 (see next chapter) as well as the incidents in 2:1-12 (the healing of the paralytic) and 3:1-6 (the healing of the withered hand) do not isolate faith as a prerequisite. Even the statement in 1:40, "If you will, you can make me clean," does not relate healing to the subjective faith of the individual, but to the will and power of Jesus.

Alan Richardson's comment on 6:5, 6a is helpful in this regard:

> Inability to perceive the true significance of His miracles was regarded by Jesus as equivalent to the rejection of His Gospel. Those who do not recognize Who Jesus is are not vouchsafed the privilege of beholding the acts of the Messiah; they have eyes which do not see, and which are not blessed by the vision

of the things which the "prophets and kings" had so long desired. This is probably the meaning of St. Mark's statement that Jesus could do no act of power in "His own country" (vi. 5). It would not have occurred to St. Mark to suppose that Jesus' power was limited by the subjective attitude of unbelief amongst the onlookers; this is a curiously modern view, based upon an unbiblical psychological theory that Jesus' healing miracles were examples of "faith-cures" (in the modern sense), which cannot be performed when "faith" i.e. a form of "suggestion") is lacking. St. Mark's own qualification—"save that He laid His hands upon a few sick folk and healed them"— ought to have been sufficient to disprove such a theory. St. Matthew has surely no intention of modifying St. Mark's statement; he merely makes St. Mark's meaning clearer: "He did not many mighty works there because of their unbelief" (xiii. 58). That is to say, Jesus refuses to show the signs of the Kingdom of God to those who will not understand them, since He does not work miracles for their own sake—either as exhibitions of power or as spontaneous deeds of compassion. The working of miracles is a part of the proclamation of the Kingdom of God, not an end in itself.[2]

Richardson's statement indicates that we should see the miracles first of all as "signs of the kingdom," and that belief/ unbelief was linked to perception of Jesus' messianic identity. The right question to ask when reading the miracles in the Gospels is *not,* "If I have enough faith, won't Jesus do a miracle for me?" *but* "From the working of the miracles already done, am I ready to affirm, without asking for more signs (see 8:11, 12), that Jesus is God's Messiah and Son, as expressly seen in his servanthood, suffering, and death?" (see chapters 7 and 10).

This precisely is the function of the mighty works in Mark's Gospel. They point to the issue ("Who is this man?") both at the beginning (4:41) and at the end (6:2, 3) of the segments: "Who then is this, that even wind and sea obey him?" The story of Jesus stilling the storm ends with that question. It may well be that in Mark's selection and joining of stories together the answer to this question cryptically comes in the next story, in 5:7, when the Gerasene demoniac, a voice from the D and D circle (see chapter 2 above) cries out, "What have you to do with me, Jesus, Son of the Most High God?" There again for those who have ears to hear and eyes to see, the answer comes, not from a human voice but from the quarters of hell!

The concluding paragraph of the segment shows again the issue prompted by the mighty works: "Where did this man get all this? What is the wisdom given to him? What mighty works are wrought by his hand! Is not this the carpenter, the son of Mary and brother of James and Joses and Judas and Simon, and are not his sisters here with us?" In effect the miracles produce the question: "Who is this man?"

This segment shows Jesus' power over four major elements of life: (1) nature, (2) demonic powers, (3) disease, and (4) death. Jesus has power over them all. What does that mean for us in our lives today as Christians? What should we learn from these stories of Jesus' power, his power over nature, his power over demons, and his power over disease and death? Let me give you a hint and a caution.

One of the emphases in Markan studies today has to do with how we correlate the first part of the Gospel with the last part of the Gospel. Specifically, how do we correlate these portraits of Jesus as a mighty wonder worker—one who performs miracles—with the latter part of the book where Jesus is the servant who suffers and dies? And even more specifically, how do we account for the fact that Mark never allows the climactic confession, "Jesus is the Son of God," to come from human lips in the context of the mighty works, but only in the context of his suffering and death, as we will see later (15:39)? Thus we are forced to come to grips with the function of the miracles in the Gospel as a whole. They certainly raise the question of who Jesus is. At the same time they do not provide the appropriate context for the answer.

What is the context in which Mark's Gospel discloses Jesus'
full power and divinity? I hope you and your study group can
struggle with this issue.

Lord God,
   when we come to Jesus' miracles,
   we need your help to understand
      their rightful role.
It's clear that they are connected to faith,
   faith in Jesus' person,
      and Jesus' power.
But we sometimes stumble on the point
      of OUR faith
      and MY cure,
   wanting either to prove your power
      by OUR faith
   or doubt your power
      by MY illness.
Open our eyes, rather, to SEE JESUS,
   and truly hear his kingdom teaching.
To expect not only miracles,
   but to experience the miracle,
   in which my (our) whole life
      is healed
         in
You, my Lord and my God.
                                    Amen.

STRUCTURAL DIAGRAM OF MARK 4:35—6:6

THE MIGHTY WORKS (6:2,5)

Jesus Stills the Sea	Jesus Heals the Gerasene Demoniac	Jesus Raises Jarius' Daughter (Heals Hemorrhage)	Rejected at Home
4:35 4:41	5:1	5:20	5:21	5:43	6:1	6:6

Contrast _____ 5:19 __ to __ 5:43 _____

Key Themes
Faith _____ 4:40 _____ 5:34, 36 _____ 6:2, 3 _____ 6:6

Jesus' Power Over:
Nature _____ Demons _____ Disease and Death

Who Is Jesus? 4:41 _____ 5:7 _____ 6:2,3

Reflection, Discussion, and Action

1. The range of Jesus' power manifested in these mighty works is impressive and overwhelming. Power over nature, demonic evil, disease, and even death. Is the purpose of Mark's telling these stories simply to tell us that Jesus worked miracles? If so, how would we compare this to other miracles reported in the ancient world?

Read Isaiah 35 and then the quotation from Alan Richardson again. What is your answer?

2. In the next lesson, we will deal more fully with how we should understand miracles and exorcism for today. But if you are studying as a group, you may want to use some time today to report on special demonstrations of God's power in the life of the church today.

3. Discuss this statement: Just as the parables teach us about the nature of the kingdom, so the mighty works show us the power of the kingdom.

4. Students sometimes get hung up on problems such as why Jesus sent the demons into the pigs and why he caused such a loss in property. While these details do indeed spice up the story, they are not central to the main point. It might be remembered, however, that the view of demons at that time assumed that when demons were exorcised they would go elsewhere, hopefully out to uninhabited areas, such as the desert or the wilderness, and stay there. Hence the demons struck quite a bargain in this case. From a Jewish point of view, however, entering into *swine* carried a touch of humor, since swine were both unclean and it was a pig that the pagan Seleucid army sacrificed on the temple altar in 168 BC, thus giving rise to the phrase, "the abomination of desolation" (see chapter 9 below). When the swine rushed headlong into the sea, they landed the demons in the home of original chaos (Genesis 1:2), but over which Jesus had already just exerted his lordship (4:35-41).

The man in the tombs in *an uninhabited place* with a le-

gion of demons (a Roman legion numbered 6,000), demons
entering swine, and swine together with demons drowning in
the sea all fit together in the thought structures of the first-
century world. The drowning of the pigs, however, represented a major economic loss to the owners, and hence their
insistence that Jesus leave the area. In this, the story contains
an evangelistic edge as well: pigs or Jesus?

5. Another question which often bothers students is
whether the man or the demons spoke in verse 7 ff. The first
century viewpoint would regard the man so possessed by the
demons that any attempt to distinguish the two is fruitless.
Since the demons took possession of the man, they spoke in
him or he spoke their words.

In the next chapter we will deal more extensively with
this topic, but it should be noted that the Gospels neither
teach demon possession nor about demon possession. They
teach deliverance from all evil, including demons. It is not important that we have a theory of demon possession, but
rather that we witness to the gospel which overcomes all evil,
regardless of how it manifests itself.

6. Since 6:1-6 functions as the climax to this segment, it
is important to note that the key question raised by this segment is *not* "What will you say about miracles?" *but* "What
will you say and do about Jesus?" The issue of belief and unbelief centers on this point.

7. Perhaps this lesson can teach us that a genuinely
Christian testimony should focus not so much on *our role* in
what God has done for us but on Jesus Christ himself and
God Almighty whom Jesus reveals. In what ways have you
claimed Christ's victory and power in your life?

Who Is This Man?

CHORIC

Who is this man
    who stands and speaks?
    . . . who speaks
    as if by his word
        the worlds are held together
    this man
        whose call
        commands
        the elements?
    this man
        who orders peace!
    this man whose word
        calls forth life
        and wholeness?
Who Is This Man?
    —thick fingers
    creased and calloused
        by adze and plane
        rasp and chisel
    gripped hard
        to shape the timbers
        of his trade?
. . . carpenter,
        bunched muscles
        rippling round
        beneath his tunic;
        builder—
    wrenched from his bench
        to shape
        a new kingdom
with carpenter as king!
Who is this man?

Who Is This Man?
  —driven into desert
    driven
    biting sand
    driven dry
  stinging
  burning sun
thirsty days
stretched across the dragging sunsets
    forty
  days burning dry
  agony
    driven into conflict
  across the landscape
   of his spirit
  every breath of victory
    near-smothered
    by the tempter's wile
      reaching
      into each human desire
      to find the hook
      of bondage
  —driven wild across the sere battle-ground
        of soul
        and purpose
  until the final triumph
  of spirit over flesh!

Who Is This Man?
  —who strikes down Lucifer
  with a Holy Word
    three times uttered
    in blaze of clashing wills;
  —who says to his underlings
    demons—OUT
    ...you may no longer live
    in human habitation!
Who Is This Man?
  —who commands the unclean spirits:

SILENCE! You may not speak,
        you must keep my secret
        that I am
        whom you know me to be—
            Son of God.

        Silence!
            you may not tell
            this secret.

Who Is This Man?
        God-man
        man-God
     touching earth with spirit
     breathing heaven
     into clods—
        whose very word
        becomes flesh;
  whose touch breath word
        grows into seeing
        into sound
        and into leaping limbs
    whose life
        gives birth
        to a new community
God-man
man-God
        touching earth with spirit
        breathing heaven
        into clods
        shaped by his hand from clay!

Who Is This Man?
       —who announces simply!
     the kingdom of God has now arrived
           who says:
        it is here
        I am—bringing it!

Who Is This Man?

        —From *To Walk in the Way*

Chapter 5

More Miracles: Their Meaning

(Mark 1:21-45)

Presession Study

1. Read Mark 1:21-45. Give titles to each paragraph on a horizontal line-portrayal.

2. Review Part I of the summary of the inductive study method in Section B of Appendix II. When you read the biblical text are you seeing *more* things now than you did when you started this study?

3. Review the features that provide structural unity to the previous three segments we studied. Can you discover which element unifies verses 21-39—persons, places, events, ideas, or time? Think hard and look carefully; this is a new type.

4. How do verses 1:40-45 relate to 1:21-39. Should they be a part of this segment or a part of the conflict stories in 2:1—3:6? Is 1:16-20 part of the segment?

5. What image or portrait of Jesus emerges from this opening snapshot of the Gospel? List particular characteristics. How does this set the stage for the whole Gospel?

6. Notice verses 25, 34, and 44. Any comments? Notice also the terms "lonely place" in verse 35 and "country" in 45. In both cases the Greek word is *erēmos,* meaning wilderness or desert. Read the introduction of the Gospel (vv. 1-13) and observe the use of the term there. With this frequent recurrence of the term in chapter 1, what might Mark be emphasizing? The exposition in chapter 6 will discuss this point.

7. What is the significance of the exorcism in the synagogue at Capernaum (vv. 21-28)? Based on this segment, how would you describe the purpose of Jesus' mission?

EXPOSITION: MARK 1:21-39 (45)

One of the striking features of Mark's Gospel is the extent to which it portrays Jesus in direct combat against evil. The story of the Gerasene demoniac, as studied in the last chapter, receives twice as much space in Mark as it does in Matthew or Luke. While Mark records at least four exorcisms,[1] John, the last Gospel written, records none. In John, Jesus' encounter with evil and triumph over evil is described in different language and situations.[2] In John's Gospel, Jesus also corrects and judges the common assumption of the time that sickness comes directly from sin (John 9:3 ff.).

Mark begins Jesus' public ministry by showing Jesus as One with authority and power over demons and disease. The segment extends from 1:21 to 1:39 (or possibly to 1:45). The segment (vv. 21-39) contains four paragraphs. The first paragraph is: *Jesus Heals a Man with an Unclean Spirit in the Capernaum Synagogue* (vv. 21-28); the second, *Jesus Heals Peter's Mother-in-law* (vv. 29-31);[3] the third, a *Mass Healing at Sundown;* and the fourth, an *Early Morning Retreat.* Whether 1:40-45, *The Healing of a Leper,* is part of this segment must be considered later. You will recognize that 2:1—3:6 is the series of *Conflict Stories* that we studied earlier.

What are the common unifying themes in 1:21-39? One prominent emphasis is Jesus' authority (1:22, 27), but this point is present also in the next segment in Jesus' conflict with Pharisaic religion. What are the emphases, themes, or features *distinctive* to this segment? What about the teaching/preaching emphasis (vv. 21, 22, 27, 38, 39) and the fact that all the paragraphs, except 35-39, tell about Jesus' "works of power," the same type of events we studied in 4:35—6:6? In this respect 1:40-45 fits nicely into the segment, but 1:35-39 does not! Is there any other feature that marks 1:21-39 off by itself, as a distinctive segment?

Thus far in the studies we have observed that *like events*

(conflict stories and mighty works) or *like ideas* (the parables) can give thematic unity to a segment. Other features which also provide structural unity are *persons, places,* or *time.* Actually, the entire Gospel is the story of one *Person,* Jesus, and this is what makes the Gospel a coherent book. Further, the Synoptic Gospels (Matthew, Mark, Luke) have similar overall place patterns—Galilee, toward Jerusalem, Jerusalem. This distinguishes the Synoptics from the fourth Gospel in which Jesus makes at least three trips to Jerusalem.

So these are examples of structural unity provided by *events, ideas, person*(s), and *places.* This segment illustrates how *time* provides structural unity. Can you see that point in the text? When did the event of each paragraph occur? It takes a little thinking, but once you notice that the mass healing occurred *"that* evening" (vv. 32-34) and the retreat took place early the next morning (vv. 35-39), it becomes clear that the healing of Peter's mother-in-law (vv. 29-31) occurred in the afternoon. Further, the "immediately" of v. 29 implies that the exorcism in the synagogue took place right before that, on sabbath morning.

What we have, therefore, in this segment is *A Day's Activity (in Capernaum).* The location is inferred, though not explicitly mentioned in all the paragraphs. Look now at the structural diagram at the end of the exposition to see how these observations are brought together and visually portrayed. How much of this did you see in your presession study?

What About 1:40-45?

It is difficult to know whether this paragraph should be considered part of 1:21-39 or 2:1—3:6. Features connecting it to 1:21-39 are:

1. It is a healing event similar to the actions of 1:21-34, but then 2:1-12 and 3:1-6 also report healing events.
2. It does emphasize Mark's secrecy theme (v. 44) al-

ready enunciated in chapter 1 (see vv. 25 and 34).

3. It also stresses Mark's interest in the *wilderness* (*erēmos,* translated also "desert" or "lonely" place) as the locale out of which Jesus' mission originates (see 1:2-13, 35, 45).[4]

But the reasons for not considering verses 40-45 part of the segment are:

1. It is not a part of the day's cycle in 1:21-39.
2. Verse 39 is itself a summary for 1:21-39.
3. Verses 40-45, like 2:1—3:6, also show Jesus' relationship to the law and the religious leaders.

In fact, Jesus' cleansing of the leper shows that Jesus fulfills what the law required but what neither the law nor its guardians, the priests, were able to produce. In this light, Jesus' healing of the leper is a fitting introduction to 2:1—3:6, for it shows that Jesus is not against the law, but that he both fulfills and transcends it in order to accomplish the good that the law ultimately intends.

In view of these considerations, it is best to regard 1:40-45 as a transitional paragraph, linking together these two segments of Mark's Gospel.

Mark's First Portrait of Jesus

Mark 1:21-39 is the Gospel's initial snapshot of Jesus— Mark's first portrait of Jesus in his public ministry. As such, Mark presents Jesus as One with great power in combat against evil. But the emphasis falls not on Jesus as a miracle-worker but upon the "authority" of Jesus and, consequently, his identity. The mood generated by this one day's snapshot is, "Who, anyway, is this man before whom the evil spirits cower and by whose word the sick are made well?"

Miracles: Then and Now

Whenever I teach Mark's Gospel, students raise the following series of questions: How should we understand the miracles in the Gospels? Do miracles happen today? Wouldn't more miracles happen if we had more faith?

In answer to these questions, it is important to keep in mind the following points:

1. Strictly speaking, the term "miracle" is not a biblical word. As the word has been used in the last several centuries, it denotes an occurrence which cannot be explained by "natural law." But people in biblical times knew nothing of natural law as we do today. In fact, the biblical terms for what we call "miracle" are signs (*semeia*), wonders, (*terrata*), works (*erga*), and powers (*dunameis*). The crucial point in these events was not whether they could or could not be explained naturally, but that they were *sign*ificant and *wonder*ful events—signs and wonders that demonstrated divine power.

2. We should guard against the modern tendency, therefore, to restrict God's acts to the "supernatural." God works through what we understand (e.g., healing through medicine) and what we don't understand (healing through anointing and prayer). Our God should not be limited to what Dietrich Bonhoeffer has called the "God of the gaps" (thinking of God as operating only *beyond* the limits of our knowledge). If this is our conception of God, then our God gets smaller as human knowledge increases. For example, while we might understand the physical processes involved in the birth of a child, we should, nonetheless, see in that event a divine power and mystery, an act significant and wonderful, even in the love that unites man and woman and functions as the context for conception.

3. We should admit that the modern tendency is to explain the "miracles." Aren't most miracles, after all, a coincidence? Didn't the first-century people misinterpret what happened? Or didn't the church create the stories for apologetic purposes? Weren't such stories simply part of the ancient worldview?

While these questions will be asked and perhaps should be asked, they nonetheless miss the intention of the biblical accounts. They betray the fact that we are imposing our criteria onto the biblical record rather than allowing the Bible to speak to us on its terms.

4. We, therefore, should seek to better understand the function and meaning of the "miracle" in the Gospels. What was the purpose and the message of "miracles"? First and foremost, the "miracles" were signs of the kingdom's advent and power, disclosures of the messianic identity of Jesus (Mark 4:41). They emphasized not the magical power of Jesus but rather the divine authority of Jesus. They authenticated the claim that Jesus came from God and was doing the work of God (John 6). In this respect, "miracles" were evidences of divine revelation. They certified the Revealer.

Further, we should note that the Gospels show great reserve in reporting miracles. When these stories are compared to other miracle stories of the time period, the distinguishing feature is not on the *power* or the effectual outcomes, but on their precise function in relation to the authority of Jesus, or later on, the Spirit's authority in the lives of the believers.

5. We must refuse the tendency to explain psychologically why miracles do or don't happen, and especially must we refuse any easy equation between sin and sickness, or making one's subjective faith the basis for healing. A healing cannot be said to be a vindication of one's faith; or, conversely, lack of healing cannot be regarded as a judgment upon the sick person. Many "miracles" in the Gospels happened apart from any statement about faith on the part of the one healed. In cases where faith or belief is prominent, the faith is commended and encouraged. But even so, the faith and belief are related to the matter of Jesus' identity, the willingness to accept him as more than ordinary man.

To reduce miracles to any easy formula of "if you believe

enough you will be healed" is to cut God down to our size, take such statements in the Bible out of the context of their original function and meaning, and overlook the importance of surprise and divine sovereignty in miracles.

6. The "miracle"-dimension of Christianity *cannot* be rightly understood if separated from the centrality of the cross and suffering. Jesus is rightly perceived to be "Son of God" through his faithful servanthood, his suffering and dying on the cross, not through his miracle-working power and deeds (Mark 15:37-39; Philippians 2:5-11; Hebrews 5:8).

As Christians we are told to copy not Jesus' miracles, but his sufferings and his self-giving love (1 Peter 2:21, 22; Ephesians 5:1, 2; cf. 1 Thessalonians 1:6, 2:14; 1 Corinthians 10:31—11:1).

Both miracle and suffering, therefore, must be seen as part of God's kingdom purpose. With the Apostle Paul, we join in creation's groaning for the full redemption of our bodies and all creation (Romans 8:18-26), knowing that "in everything God works for good with those who love him" and nothing shall "separate us from the love of God in Christ Jesus our Lord" (Romans 8:27-39).

Is healing in the atonement? Yes, but so are suffering and death. Further, not all the healing dividends are paid in this life, but in the full redemption of the life to come. The Christian emphasis falls upon suffering and death as the means by which healing is achieved.

7. The Christian's major concern is not about miracles and/or demons, *but God*. Our thoughts and actions must be God-oriented. There is truth in Karl Barth's line that when you know God's power and action, you "can wink at the devil," because you know his doom is sure, his threats passing.

Jesus' Victory Over Satan
Before looking specifically at the issue of exorcism, the

casting out of demons, and our Christian response, we should observe the prominent role and significance of Jesus' encounter with Satan and evil in Mark's Gospel. Numerous scholarly studies have focused on the subject.[5] There is general agreement that Mark emphasizes the view that Jesus' ministry is an attack upon Satan's dominion and a plundering of his possessions, so clearly described in the Beelzebul controversy (3:22-27). Ernest Best holds that the decisive battle was fought and won in the temptation (1:12, 13) when the Spirit literally impelled Jesus into the wilderness for combat against evil.[6] The public ministry was then a mopping up after the victory. The victory in Jesus' temptation was the binding of the strong man, Satan (3:27), and the public ministry was the plundering of his house—snatching people and creation (4:35-41) away from his grasp (3:27).

Another writer on the subject, Ulrich Mauser, observes that the wilderness locale functions as a type of headquarters for Jesus' ministry. One significant aspect of this was Jesus' attack upon and victory over the demons, who also headquartered in the wilderness. Another contribution, that of James Robinson, portrays the contest taking place in Jesus' ministry, but consummated through the cross and resurrection.[8] As Best points out, however, Mark does not emphasize Satan's role in the passion, not even in Judas. Rather, Jesus' *tempters (peirazein)* in Mark are Satan (1:12, 13), the Pharisees (8:11; 10:2; 12:15), and, by inference, Peter (8:32, 33).

Since Jesus, in his sharp rebuke to Peter, specifically identifies Peter's resistance to his suffering and death as satanic (8:33), the dispute merits our careful notice of the crucial difference between Jesus and Satan. As we will see in chapters 7 and 8, Jesus' view of messiahship includes suffering and cross; Peter, following Jewish messianic hopes, expected the Messiah to be a military hero wielding triumphant political power. *Such* messiahship Jesus refuses, calling it the satanic model.

Jesus' attack upon Satan's dominion, therefore, is all in-
clusive: both the exorcisms and the call to suffering discipleship free people from Satan's oppression. Christians today
are called to wage battle against the same evils, evils that op-
press and rob people of God's intended freedom and wholeness.

It may be true that current psychiatric practice would
classify some cases of first-century demon possession as
mental illness.[9] But the larger point we should see in these
stories is that Jesus releases people from all bondage, and
especially those forms of satanic bondage that the Pharisees
and Peter represented. Hence, we should not focus on demon
possession in any narrow sense, but seek to combat all evil
through the power of Jesus Christ. The task of Christ's community is to claim Jesus' victory and power and thus serve as
agents of healing and wholeness in all dimensions of life.

What About Casting Out Demons?

On exorcisms and demon possession, we should keep in
mind all of the above and note further:

1. That such thinking and action as described in the Gospels takes place regularly in many non-Western cultures today.

2. That such thinking and action (including reputed
exorcisms) permeated various cultures of the first-century
world.

3. That comparatively speaking, the New Testament
shows restraint in this emphasis as it does also in reporting
other miracles, especially in the later Gospels and Paul's writings.

4. That "demons" and "possession," represent one type
of linguistic description of the reality of evil; but there are
also other vocabulary sets: "the works of the flesh," "the
principalities and the powers," and even more cryptic images
in Revelation.

5. That the permanent Christian task is to combat evil in all its forms. We should be cautious that we do not:

(a) Focus too narrowly on one form of "demon possession" (which is likely rare in the culture in which we live) and then fail to see evil (the demonic forces) at work in the human sins of greed, power, oppression of the weak and poor, and other social ills which permeate all levels of economic and political life.

(b). Quench the power of the Spirit in the use of gifts and stifle God's goal of overcoming all evil by the resurrection power of his Son.

6. Our emphasis should be on Christ's victory over evil and *his* power to help us live in freedom from control of all evil.

7. Not the devil, but God is the focus of Christian living.

Almighty God,
    we acknowledge your sovereign power,
        power over all evil,
        power to free us from every oppression, and
        power to make us new beings.
May we be so overcome with your presence
    that our lives will be filled
        with joy and gladness, and
        with triumph and power.
Help us to be bold witnesses for your kingdom
    so that evil may be crushed
        by the word of truth, and
        by the sword of the Spirit.
We praise You
    that through Jesus Christ
    we are more than conquerors,
    and that nothing,
        not even demons or death,
    can separate us from your love
        in Jesus Christ our Lord.   *Amen.*

STRUCTURAL DIAGRAM OF 1:20-39 (45)

A DAY'S ACTIVITY IN CAPERNAUM

Heals Man with Unclean Spirit in Capernaum Synagogue	Heals Peter's Mother-in-law	Mass Healing at Sundown	Early Morning Retreat	Heals a Leper
1:21 1:28	1:29 1:31	1:32 1:34	1:35 1:39	1:40 1:45

Summary v.39

Time Structure: One Day
(morning) ———— (afternoon) ———— "that evening" ———— "early morning"

Key Themes
authority
vv. 22 ———— 27

teaching/preaching
vv. 21,22 ———— 27   38, 39

healing/exorcism
vv. 24-26 ———— 30, 31 ———— 34 ———— 39

secrecy
vv. 25 ———— 34 ———— 44

wilderness (*erēmos*)
35 ———— 45

Reflection, Discussion, and Action

1. I expect this chapter and topic will generate much discussion in your study group. In his book Paul M. Miller says, "I feel that Christ's exorcisms were signs of His kingdom's inbreaking, and that the church need not struggle to duplicate them any more than His stilling of the storm, raising of Lazarus, or turning the water into wine."[10] What do you think? It will be a healthy sign if you discover that neither you nor I have all the answers to the questions that come up. On the issue of miracles especially, I think it is important for us to have an attitude of humility and to remain open to God's surprises!

2. Discuss the following statement: Christians today suffer from two maladies, both extremes. Some too easily give God and/or Satan credit or blame for everything in an almost casual, flippant way while others seldom or never relate the course of life's affairs to either Satan or God.

3. Why after such a successful day's activity did Jesus retreat to the wilderness? Notice the fresh directive of verse 38. What is the relationship between the "mighty works" and the preaching?

4. In verse 41, most translations say Jesus was "moved with pity." A few early and quite reliable manuscripts, however, say he was "moved with anger." What does your version say? Even though on manuscript evidence alone, the choice would clearly be "pity," it is then very difficult to explain how some scribes would have written "anger." On the other hand, if it was originally "anger," it is easy to imagine how and why copyists would change it to "pity." I think it is likely that the original text said "anger." Jesus was moved to anger when he saw the terrible effects of leprosy, not only physical, but also social—ostracized as the leper was from the community. The questioning of Jesus' desire to heal in the face of the illness' ravaging effect upon the outcast triggered Jesus' "warm indignation" (*The New English Bible's*

ingenious blending of the two texts!). Jesus' healing of the leper was thus also a victory over Satan's house.

5. In verse 35 we are told that Jesus prayed. Can you sense his need for depending on the Father's guidance and power, even after the divine affirmation as "Son of God" (1:11) and his victory over Satan (1:13)? What role does prayer play in your life? What does prayer say about our attitude toward ourselves and toward God?

6. I expect that you feel you sometimes have more to do in one day than is reasonable. But did you think about all Jesus did in one day (1:21-39) and how draining such activity was? At the center of Jesus' work and authority was the assurance of doing God's will and work. Discuss with each other how your days' work can better reflect doing the Father's business.

7. Caring, helping, praying, claiming divine power over evil, standing for the right, and teaching kingdom values are directives we've received thus far from Mark's Gospel. Do these themes characterize our lives as we follow Jesus?

If you are studying in a group, I advise that you take two sessions for chapter 6, including this review, as well as the exam, the reflection, the recapitulation, and the learning dialogue at the end of chapter 6.

REVIEW AND OVERVIEW (BOAT RIDE I)

1. Aside from the introduction to the Gospel (1:1-15), we have now studied everything in the Gospel up to 6:30 except 1:16-20, 3:7-35, and 6:6-29. Read these passages and note that each one contains the same theme. What is it?

2. In fact, if we regard 3:7-12 as a summary paragraph at the end of the preceding two segments (the *Day's Activity* and the *Conflict Stories*), then each one of these three passages either focuses totally on that theme (1:16-20) or begins with it. What is the function of this recurring theme in the unity and structure of the book?

3. *After* you've exhausted the insights of your own observations turn to the next page and study the structural portrayal of this first third of the Gospel. Note the observations and comments. If the smaller units in the closed rectangles are segments, what are the next larger units called—from 1:16 to 3:12 and 3:13 to 6:6b? See Appendix II, Section B.

STRUCTURAL PORTRAYAL OF 1:16—6:30

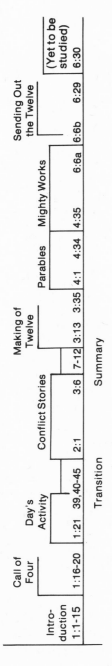

Intro- duction	Call of Four	Day's Activity		Conflict Stories		Making of Twelve		Parables		Mighty Works		Sending Out the Twelve		
1:1-15	1:16-20	1:21	39, 40-45	2:1	3:6	7-12	3:13	3:35	4:1	4:34	4:35	6:6a	6:6b	6:29
		Transition		Summary										(Yet to be studied) 6:30

Observations and Comments

1. This first part of the Gospel contains four well-unified segments (in the rectangles), but 1:16-20; 3:13-35; and 6:6b-29 (as we will see) are not a part of those segments.

2. These verses (in 1 above) contain a similar thematic emphasis, namely, a focus on the role of the disciples. In each case the disciples emerge with more importance and responsibility in Jesus' ministry. What does this type of structure say about Mark's overall emphasis and his view of the role of the disciples?

3. Verses 13-35 are especially crucial because they not only show the emergence of the twelve as a permanent group (to whom Jesus entrusts "the secret of the kingdom" in 4:10, 11), but they also declare that Jesus' ministry is the defeat of Satan (3:20-27), that identifying Jesus' ministry as demonically inspired is unforgiveable blasphemy against the Holy Spirit (28-30), and that normal family relationships are eclipsed by a new definition of family—"Whoever does the will of God is my brother, and sister, and mother" (31-35).

4. Just as 3:13-35 clearly shows the emergence of a new reality and community around Jesus, so 6:6b-29 shows the potential missionary extension of that community and records the end of the "forerunner" period (John's death). As we begin 6:30, *Jesus and his disciples* (here called "apostles"—those with a special commission) are now the central characters of the Gospel narrative, and will continue so until 10:52.

Chapter 6

Jesus Feeds the Multitudes: The Disciples' Breakthrough

(Mark 6:30–8:30)

Presession Study

1. Until now we have devoted one chapter to each segment in Mark, but beginning with this chapter we will focus on one entire *section* in each chapter. Did you get the answer to question 3 in the Review and Overview?

2. Read 6:30—8:30. What are the two main events, one at the beginning and the other toward the end, of this section of Mark (6:30—8:30)? Actually each of these events is also a double (or perhaps triple) cycle of events. What is the triple sequence of events in each of these cycles (6:30-52 and 8:1-17)?

a. First, Jesus_____.

b. Second, Jesus takes his disciples for a_____.

c. Third, the discussion or comments of the text focus on the disciples' failure to _____
As structural units, each of these cycles should be considered_____, defined as a number of paragraphs showing structural unity (see Appendix II, Section B).

3. Chapter 7 comes between these two main events. At

first it seems unrelated, but as we shall see, it is very much related to the cycles in chapters 6 and 8. Probably 7:1-23 and 24-37 should be considered two separate segments. Why? What are the themes and moods of these two segments? Any *contrasts?* What term recurs six times in 7:1-13?

4. Two key words recur frequently and at crucial places throughout this entire section. Are you able to find them? (KJV translates the one even in 7:2 and 5 which the RSV unfortunately omits in translation.) In what way do these two terms build the pressure of the secret and put us into the very middle of the unfolding drama of the Gospel?

5. Where did the two feedings take place? Note the emphasis in 6:30-35. Compare this with 1:3, 4, 12, 13, 35, 45. What happened in such a place in the Old Testament? For how long? What did Israel eat during that time? Any lights going on? Note Hosea 2:14 ff. and John 6:31-35.

6. What really is Jesus wanting his disciples to understand in the "boat exam" in 8:14-21? Is there any significance to the numbers?

7. Read Mark 8:22-26. Isn't it odd that Jesus touched the blind man's eyes twice before he saw clearly? What else happened twice in this section (6:30—8:21)? Any connection? Read 8:27-30? What finally happens? Who sees? For the first time in the Gospel, ———————————————————.
If *you* see all things clearly, you don't need to read the exposition!

EXPOSITION: MARK 6:30–8:30

The study of this chapter takes us to the early center of Mark's Gospel; the next two chapters will take us to the later and crucial center. After the mighty works in 4:35—6:6 the disciples come back onto center stage in the Gospel. In 6:7-13, Jesus calls to himself the twelve and sends them out two by two. Jesus commissions them to do the work of the kingdom. After Mark presents the parables of the kingdom, he shows the power of the kingdom in the mighty works; and now he narrates how Jesus sent out the disciples to do the work of the kingdom. In this context we are reminded that John the Baptist has been beheaded; the "forerunner" period has ended (6:14-29).

It's interesting how Mark's Gospel handles the role of John the Baptist. In 1:14, after John was arrested, Jesus came into Galilee preaching the gospel of the kingdom of God. Jesus' public ministry is tied sequentially to what happened to John. It begins when John was arrested, and now at this critical point it is carried forward by Jesus' followers in the context of John's death. So now the new community, the kingdom community, is on center stage, with John, the forerunner of that community, gone from the scene. After the disciples' "field experience" in kingdom work, Jesus takes the twelve (in verse 30 called "apostles") into the wilderness.

The Content of the Section

Mark appears to make a special point of the wilderness, mentioning it three times in verses 31-35. It's a little difficult to locate this phrase because sometimes it's translated "lonely place," sometimes it's translated "desert," and sometimes it's translated "wilderness" (in 1:45 the RSV translates it "country"). In the Greek text, however, the same word occurs in three related forms (*erēmos, erēmia,* or *erēmos topos*), with *topos* meaning "place." In this one paragraph, Mark uses "wilderness place" (*erēmos topos*) each of the three times; "Come away by yourselves to a lonely place, and rest awhile" (v. 31); "And they went away in the boat to a lonely place" (v. 32), and again, "And when it grew late, his disciples came to him and said, 'This is a lonely place, and the hour is now late; send them away, to go into the country and villages round about and buy themselves something to eat' " (v. 35). While Mark mentions the lonely place (wilderness) three times in this one setting, Matthew mentions it only twice (14:13, 15), and Luke only once (9:12). It appears that the wilderness setting is significant to Mark.

Next comes the story of Jesus feeding the five thousand. The story itself extends from verses 30-44 (read it quickly in your Bible). As you notice in verse 41, Jesus took

the five loaves and two fish ... looked up to heaven, and blessed, and broke the loaves, and gave them to the disciples to set before the people; and he divided the two fish among them all. And they all ate and were satisfied. And they took up twelve baskets full of broken pieces and of the fish. And those who ate the loaves were five thousand men.

Look now at verse 45. The feeding is followed by a boat ride for the disciples. Interesting, isn't it? You get your meal out in the desert and then you go for a boat ride!

While on the boat ride a dramatic experience occurred. When the disciples were out on the boat and Jesus was alone on the land,

he saw that they were making headway painfully,[1] for the wind was against them. And about the fourth watch of the night he came to them, walking on the sea. He meant to pass by them, but when they saw him walking on the sea they thought it was a ghost, and cried out; for they all saw him, and were terrified. But immediately he spoke to them and said, "Take heart, it is I; have no fear." And he got into the boat with them and the wind ceased. And they were utterly astounded, for they did not understand about the loaves, but their hearts were hardened.

Only one translation, as far as I know, renders verse 50 as powerfully as it should be. It's the Amplified Version which reads, "Take heart. I AM" (*egō eimi*). The Greek has the same term as occurs in the Greek translation (Septuagint) of Exodus 3:14 in Yahweh's self-revelation to his people; "I AM WHO I AM." In Mark we are face-to-face with a divine epiphany. Jesus identifies himself to the disciples with this revered, holy, sacred name, "I AM." And they are utterly astounded!

What do people do when they are in the presence of the divine? In Mark they are amazed, astounded, and filled with fear and astonishment.[2] The text indicates that they were "utterly astounded" and then it says that *the reason* they were astounded is *because* they did not understand about the bread. That seems to indicate that if they had understood about the bread they wouldn't have been astounded at the *ego eimi,* the "I AM" revelation. But they didn't understand what was going on in the bread. Do you?!

In chapter 8 we have a second similar cycle: Jesus feeds the multitude, takes his disciples on a boat ride, and then focuses the discussion on understanding. But again the disciples don't understand. Do you?!

Sandwiched between these two similar events, chapter 7 shows two kinds of responses to Jesus. Did you identify these two contrasting responses in your presession study? How do they compare? Who are the two groups? As I'll point out later, the theme of bread (loaves) runs right through chapter 7 and thus unifies this entire section. This section is the bread-section of Mark. *The key themes are bread and understanding.*

Let's look at the second feeding in chapter 8. It begins by noting that Jesus had compassion on the crowds because they had been with him for three days and had nothing to eat. Again in verse 4 we read: "How can one feed these men with bread here in the desert?" *the wilderness (erēmia).* This time the disciples located only seven loaves and a few small fish for

four thousand. But after the feeding they took up the broken
pieces and seven baskets were left over!
Then immediately they go again for a boat ride (vv. 10,
13). Jesus sent the crowd away and made ready to go for
another boat ride with his disciples, but before they push off
shore, Pharisees come and want a sign. It's getting pretty
intense, even for the Pharisees! They want a sign! Where were
they anyway when the multitude was fed? Asking for a sign
now? What were they doing? Didn't they see what Jesus had
just done?

Then Jesus and his disciples push off for another boat
ride, this time with an intense final grueling examination! The
disciples raise the topic of bread again, complaining that they
have only one loaf along. Jesus then warns his disciples
against the "leaven of the Pharisees and the leaven of
Herod," referring apparently to the unbelief of the Pharisees
portrayed in verse 12. The disciples' mind-set is: *one* loaf for
twelve of us? *Twelve men* eat more than one loaf of bread! But
Jesus, being aware of their thinking (v. 17)

> said to them, "Why do you discuss the fact that you have no
> bread? Do you not yet perceive or understand? Are your hearts
> hardened? Having eyes do you not see, and having ears do you
> not hear? And do you not remember? When I broke the five
> loaves for the five thousand, how many baskets full of broken
> pieces did you take up? They said to him, "Twelve." "And the
> seven for the four thousand, how many baskets full of broken
> pieces did you take up?" And they said to him, "Seven." And
> he said to them, "Do you not yet understand?"

Do you not *yet* understand? Do you *understand*? Do *you*
understand?

Look, this is now the second boat ride. There were also
two feedings. After the first feeding the disciples were "utterly
astounded" at the divine epiphany because they didn't understand about the loaves, the bread. In that case five loaves fed
five thousand people and twelve baskets were left over. In the

second feeding seven loaves fed four thousand and seven baskets were left over. Do you understand? Do you know the secret? As I indicated, two key themes run through this entire section. The one is the word "bread." This term occurs seventeen times; in 6:37, 38, 41 (twice), 44, 52. It may be translated "bread" or "loaves"; it is always the same in Greek, the word, *artos.* In Mark 7 it occurs three times. The first part of chapter 7 says that the Pharisees will not eat bread. While the KJV translates the term in verses 2 and 5 the RSV simply says "eat" and thus misses the emphasis on "bread." Mark's point is that they will not eat *bread* until they wash their hands.[3] In contrast to the Pharisees, the Syrophoenician woman (v. 27) begs for the crumbs of *bread* dropping from the table. Here is the clue for understanding how chapter 7 functions, sandwiched as it is between the bread feedings.

Chapter 7 thus presents first the negative response of the Pharisees (vv. 1-23) who because of their traditions (used six times), like laborious washing of hands, refused to accept the signs of the feedings (see 8:10-12), whereas the Gentiles (vv. 24 ff. and 31 ff.) received with open arms and hearts the power which disclosed who Jesus is!

In chapter 8 Mark uses the term bread three times (8:4, 5, 6) to introduce the feeding. Then on the boat ride we have bread, bread, bread: 8:14 (twice), 8:16, 8:17, 8:19. Thus, the entire section is about "bread," with heavy emphasis on bread right at the end.

Do you know what the bread is about? If you do, then you also *understand,* Mark's other key term which occurs in 6:52, 7:14, 7:18, and 8:17. In the Greek text it is the very last word of the paragraph ending in verse 21. It concludes with the word, *suniete.* Do you "understand"? The bread is intended to lead to understanding—for the disciples then and for us as readers now.

Look now at the structural diagram at the end of the exposition for a visual portrayal of the content and emphases of the section.

Understanding the Section
In Mark 4 the emphasis fell upon *hearing* and *understanding*. Note the similarity between 4:10-12 and 8:17, 18! In Mark 8—10 we will see continuing emphasis on understanding. What's going on? What's going on in the *bread?* What must be understood?

Observe, first of all, that Mark emphasizes Jesus' retreat into the wilderness or the desert as the setting for this section (6:30-35). Do you recall anything from your Old Testament knowledge about the significance of the wilderness and the desert? Mark's Gospel begins with quotations from Malachi and from Isaiah. The one from Isaiah reads, "The voice of one crying *in the wilderness:* Prepare the way of the Lord, make his paths straight" (italics mine). Further in chapter 1 John was *in the wilderness* preaching (1:4) and Jesus was *in the wilderness,* tempted by Satan (1:13). Jesus also retreated twice into the wilderness (1:35, 45). The wilderness connotes important theological meaning in the Gospel of Mark.

Hosea 2:14 ff. says, in looking beyond Israel's broken covenant with Yahweh, there will come a day when I (God) will take you back again *into the wilderness* and there we'll have another honeymoon! It will be as in the days of old and I will make a covenant with you, a betrothal to you in justice, righteousness, steadfast love, mercy, and faithfulness. The *wilderness* will be the setting in which the messianic hope is fulfilled!

Not only did the Old Testament prophets view the wilderness as the headquarters, the context out of which the messianic age would emerge, but the Qumran community located itself in the wilderness east of Jerusalem. And for what reason? In their *Manual of Discipline* they tell us they went *into the wilderness* to prepare for the way of the Lord. "To prepare the way of the Lord" meant getting ready for the coming Messiah and they believed he would emerge in the wilderness. One of the intertestamental books says,

> And it shall come to pass at that self-same time [when the Messiah appears] that the treasury of manna shall again descend from on high, and they will eat of it in those years, because they have come to the consummation of time.[4]

And one of the Sibylline Oracles, written in the first century BC or AD says that manna is expected to be the food of the members of the messianic kingdom.[5]

In view of these texts it is clear that one of the expected signs of the Messiah was opening the windows of heaven and raining down manna as in the days of Moses. Little wonder then that the feeding of the multitudes functions so pivotally in the unfolding of the secret in Mark's Gospel. Do *you* know what's going on in the bread?

In John's parallel (6:30-35), the Pharisees discuss with Jesus the meaning of the bread. The discussion is intense. They want a sign, but they refuse to admit the significance of what they already saw! They remind Jesus that Moses supplied bread for forty years and . . .? Couldn't you keep that bread coming? We need a sign! That's the implication of the dialogue. But because of their hardness of heart, they did not comprehend what was to be seen in these two bread feedings.

Immediately after Jesus examines his disciples on the boat ride, a most unusual event occurs in 8:22-26. Jesus heals a blind man by touching his eyes twice. This is the sixth occurrence of things coming in two: two feedings, two boat rides, two sets of numbers (five and twelve, four and seven), two types of response in chapter 7, and two sides of the sea. The story takes place at Bethsaida, located at the north edge of the Sea of Galilee and midway between the west and east sides of the sea.

Geography: Do You Understand?

A lesson in geography will help us understand. On the map below note where the solid line ends and the dotted line begins. Note also that all the events from 7:24 to 8:10 happen in dotted line areas. Who lives in the dotted line areas? Who lives in the solid line areas?

Now correlate the geography with the two types of response in chapter 7, with the "two-pattern" developed in this section, and with the numbers for the two feedings: west side, five and twelve; east side, four and seven. Do you understand?

Notice also that Caesarea Philippi is located on the border east and west, north and south. Here where Palestine touches the pagan Gentile world Jesus is confessed _____! Think about the significance of that. Are you beginning to see (with your eyes touched twice) how centrally the mission to the Gentiles functions in Mark's Gospel?

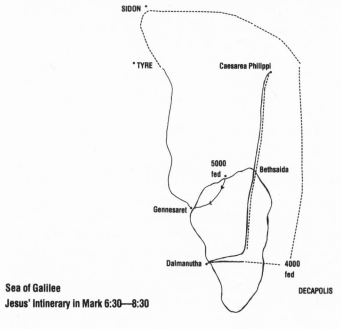

Sea of Galilee
Jesus' Intinerary in Mark 6:30—8:30

O God, here we are,
        fed and touched,
        at the threshold
                With insight about to break.
We saw you, Jesus,
        cast out the unclean spirits,
        heal the sick,
        cure the leper,
and put human need above law and tradition.
We heard you, Jesus,
        teach about the kingdom,
        announce its arrival,
                its growth,
                and its sure consummation.
And we saw the kingdom power
        in the stilling of the storm,
        in the liberated demoniac,
        in the healed hemorrhage,
        and in the resurrection from death.
Who are you, Jesus?
        feeding the multitudes,
                not once, but twice,
        touching blind eyes,
                not once, but twice.
                Bringing bread and sight to all!
You took us into the wilderness,
        like Israel of old;
        there you fed us manna.
        You became our bread.
                And the boat rides we'll never forget.
        The EGO EIMI, and
                the hard quizzing,
                twelve—five, seven—four,
        No, Jesus, we won't forget.
But, Jesus, who are you?
        one of the scribes?   *No.*
        of Beelzebub?   *No.*
Jesus, who are you?
                Do we know?
                Do we understand?
                Do we see clearly?
Help us, O God.
        for Jesus' sake.   *Amen.*

STRUCTURAL DIAGRAM: MARK 6:30—8:30

	Feeding Cycle 1					Responses				Feeding Cycle 2				
					Jewish			Gentile						

Feeding Cycle 1

Feeding 5,000	Boat Ride	Sum-mary
6:30 6:44	6:45 52	6:53 56

Epiphany and Understanding

Responses

Jewish

Traditions	Inner and Outer	Syrophoe-nician Woman
7:1 7:13	7:14 7:23	7:24 7:30

Gentile

Decapolis Deaf Man
7:31 7:37

Feeding Cycle 2

Feeding 4,000	Pharisees Ask for Sign	Boat Ride
8:1 8:10	8:11 13	8:14 21

Do you under-stand?

Blind Man of Bethsaida	Great Confession
8:22 26	27 30

Key Themes

Bread (used 17 times)
6:37, 38, 41, 44 — 52 ——— 7:2 —— 5 ————— 27 ————— 8:4, 5, 6. ——————— 14, 15, 16, 17, 19

Understanding
—————— 6:52 ————— 7:14, 18 ——————————— 8:17, 21

Reflection, Discussion, and Action

1. Today you are left on the borderline between 8:26 and 8:27 of the Gospel. You are standing at the midpoint, Bethsaida, with the blind man about to receive sight! For your discussion I would like you to grapple intensely with what's really going on at this point in the Gospel. From what has been said, it should be clear to you by now that the feeding of the multitudes is indeed the supreme messianic sign. It happened twice: first, five loaves for five thousand and then seven loaves for four thousand with twelve and seven loaves respectively left over. Are these numbers significant? I don't usually make much of numbers in the Bible but when Jesus takes his disciples on a boat ride and quizzes them about certain numbers, then I want to know if they are significant and I think you also will want to know. Do you understand?

I'll give a couple hints:

Hint 1: If you observe the text carefully, you will note that the first feeding was on the west side of the sea, the second on the east side.

Hint 2: Chapter 7 is sandwiched between the two feedings and shows two kinds of responses.

Hint 3: It takes two touches to make the blind man see.

Do you know the meaning of the bread and do you understand? Are the numbers significant? Your study group should wrestle with this emphasis in the biblical text. And each of you should search, think, and pray about it until the next study session.

2. In my classroom teaching, students often answer the above questioning as follows: "The disciples are supposed to understand that Christ is the bread of life." Then I say, "No, no, no. You're giving John's answer to Mark's question. What is the answer on Mark's terms?" First, note that the first part to the answer, "Christ is . . ." shows that the student

knows the answer but forgot the question with which the disciples struggled in Mark's Gospel. Second, the last part of the answer, ". . . the bread of life," is a spiritualized statement characteristic of John's Gospel, but not Mark's. Mark's emphasis upon Jesus' bread for the multitudes focuses rather on (1) the _____ of Jesus (8:27-30), and (2) the inclusion of_____ and _____ in the banquet that Jesus, the _____ provides (recall the two sides of the sea and the groups responding in chapter 7).

3. We have heard it said: no Christ, no mission. But Mark's point is even more striking. By showing that the Gentiles must be included into God's blessings before Jesus is confessed to be the Messiah, Mark's Gospel says: no mission, no Christ? As you study the next chapter, note how Jesus could not accept the politically exclusivistic Jewish view of messiahship.

Might this help us understand why Mark allows Jesus' messianic identity to be confessed only in the context of showing that the kingdom is for both Jews and Gentiles? Further, I suggest that this also helps us to understand better Mark's secrecy theme. It cannot be told unless it is clear that Jesus is Messiah for all people!

4. Taking chapter 7 as a mirror of different kinds of responses to Jesus, how would you compare these responses to those of your own life and to those of your congregation?

Write your answers below:

REVIEW AND EXAM (BOAT RIDE II)

At this juncture in the study of the Gospel a thorough review is in order, solidifying the gains of your first boat ride where we focused on an overview of chapters 1-6, which can now be extended to chapter 8.

1. Write down five major thematic emphases of Mark's Gospel that you have observed thus far.

    a.   d.

    b.   e.

    c.

2. List all the verses that reflect emphasis on secrecy.

_____

Why does Jesus command people not to tell? _____

_____

_____

3. What is the secret in the Gospel? _____

How is it disclosed? _____

_____

4. List all verses and/or events that build the question, Who is Jesus?

_____

_____

Can anything be left out?! Which verses and who answer the

question?_____

_____

5. Can you recite in rapid sequence the segment title and paragraph titles for each of the following?

1:21-45 _____

2:1–3:6 _____

4:1-34 _____

4:35–6:6 _____

6. What are the main events in the segments in the section we just studied, 6:30—8:30? What does Jesus want the disciples to understand? Five and twelve, four and seven—do *you* understand?

_____

_____

7. Why is 8:27-30 called the watershed or crucial point of the Gospel?

_____

_____

_____

_____

REFLECTION

When the Messiah comes
 he will open the windows of heaven
 and rain down manna,
  as in the days of Moses.
In the wilderness,
 five loaves with 5000 fed and filled,
 and twelve baskets left over.
A boat ride,
 disciples tossing at sea,
 fighting the wind at the oars;
  a form appears
  Ego Eimi: I Am!
 the sea is calm,
 the disciples are astounded!
  Because *they did not understand*
  about the loaves.
Again, in the wilderness,
 on the other side,
 seven loaves with 4000 fed and filled,
 and seven baskets left over.
Another boat ride,
 and a grueling examination,
  quizzing on bread
  quizzing on numbers
   Do *you understand?*
A blind man comes,
 Jesus touches his eyes once—
  he sees men like trees walking;
   Will he *ever see?*
 Jesus touches a *second* time—
  and he *sees* all things clearly!
   Do *you see* clearly?

RECAPITULATION

I gave you some puzzles to work on in the last study and probably your comments have been, "I don't think we understand yet." Do you remember the hints? *Two* feedings occurred on *two* sides of the sea; Mark 7 depicted *two* contrasting responses; and finally the blind eyes were opened by *two* touches. Seeing what should be seen in the feedings parallels the outcome of two touches of the blind eyes. *To see who Jesus is, is to receive sight.*

I also asked you to think about the numbers. The first feeding was on the west side of the Sea of Galilee. Five loaves fed five thousand, with twelve baskets left over. The second feeding occurred on the other side of the sea, as far as we can determine from the text. As in the case of the healing of the Gerasene demoniac, it was located in Gentile territory. In that feeding seven loaves fed four thousand, and seven baskets were left over. Then on the second boat ride, Jesus presses for understanding, "Do you understand, do you know?"

Sandwiched between these events, Mark 7 shows us two kinds of responses. The first part of the chapter may be connected with the first feeding, thus showing us the response of the Pharisees, the response of Judaism, by and large, to the coming of Jesus as Messiah. The second part of Mark 7 occurred not in Palestine, but in Syrophoenicia and Decapolis respectively. Since Decapolis was located east of the Sea of Galilee, both of these events occurred in Gentile regions. Significantly, these responses from Gentiles were positive.

A LEARNING DIALOGUE

Teacher
Now for the numbers: what
might *twelve* symbolize? What
might five symbolize? Surely
you know, at least many of you,
what twelve symbolizes in the
Old Testament?

Students
The number of the tribes of
Israel. And, indeed, we also
learned that Jesus did choose
(or make, create) *twelve* disciples
(apostles), creating a new Israel
to carry forward his mission
(Mark 3:13-19). So twelve
represents the people of God.

The *whole* people of God?
Don't forget we have a second
feeding, and the number *seven!*
But for now, let's stick to the
first feeding. What about *five?*
Does it have symbolic significance?
I don't know, five and seven,
of course, make twelve, but. . . .

But think, put on your Old
Testament glasses. What was the
foundation upon which Israel, God's
people, based its faith and hope?
The five books of Moses?
The Pentateuch?

Right, you are. The Pentateuch, known as the Torah, formed

the foundation for Israel's life,
beliefs, and hopes. The community
was to be built upon Torah. Torah
was bread and life, the foundation
of their being.

> But twelve and five have signifi-
> cance primarily in the Jewish
> context. . . .

Indeed so, and they occur in
only the first feeding—on the *west*
side of the sea—in Jewish territory.
What are the numbers in the second
feeding?

> Seven and four.

And on which side of the sea?

> The east side, apparently.

So what might be the significance of the seven loaves and the
seven baskets left over? Does
seven occur elsewhere in the
Bible?

> The seven days of creation and the
> seven churches in Revelation.

Yes, and creation, of course,
refers to creation of the whole world.
Adam and Eve head up *all*
humanity, not just Israel.
Further, the seven churches were
located where?

> Asia Minor, where the population
> *was predominantly Gentile.*

So seven, the number of per-
fection, or better, the universal
number, points us to the Gentiles—
hence the bread for *all* people.
But what about four?

Ah, yes, the *four Gospels,* the
foundation of the new Israel, the
church of Jesus Christ, including
Jews *and Gentiles.*

But, when Mark wrote, the
four Gospels were not written yet,
so . . .?
                    I goofed.

However, Irenaeus, a
second-century church father,
says that in the divine providence the four Gospels became
the Scripture of the church—no
more and no less—and why?
                    One for each season of the year?

No, no . . . Irenaeus says,
*one Gospel for each of the four
corners of the earth.* The four
Gospels symbolize the universal-
ity of the Christian gospel.
                    So you're suggesting that the seven
                    and the four mark the feeding east
                    of the sea as a feeding for the
                    Gentiles and the five/twelve
                    feeding west of the sea is for the
                    Jews.

Yes, and don't forget that
east of the sea is Gentile
territory. But, even more specifically, I suggest that both
feedings together disclose *who
Jesus is,* since, when the
Messiah comes, *he* not only
restores the manna of Moses, but
he extends God's blessings to
(through) Israel to the whole
world. "All the nations shall . . . come
. . ." (Isaiah 2:2c) and "all shall
know me" (Jeremiah 31:34b).

We Have Seen His Power

CHORIC
We have seen his power
We have felt his touch
We have known his breath upon us
        but even though
        that day was glad
        which brought to us
        deliverance
                —there is more
                much more—
he has become our king
lord of our spirits
        Great Spirit
        Father God
        come in flesh
        as Son
                to make his kingdom
                here—
                among men
                        and we—
his early subjects
sharply brought to faith
by acts of Jesus-power,
it is true
                        —have gone beyond:
                our vision reaches far beyond
                the elements
                from which we're made
                and which we walk upon
. . . to his kingdom
                      which
        by his Spirit
        is born

and grows
in hearts of those
who follow him
and make for him
a place
to rule
and finish

all his purpose.

—From *To Walk in the Way*

Part II

THE KINGDOM WAY

"If any man would come after me,
let him deny himself
and take up his cross
and follow me"

Chapter 7

Jesus Teaches Discipleship

(Mark 8:27—10:52)

Presession Study

1. Read 8:27—10:52. This passage is one section with several segments, as was 6:30—8:30. Can you isolate the segments within the section?

2. Can you identify any recurring themes or emphases? What *new* themes emerge in this part of the Gospel? What happens three times?

3. If you have located Jesus' statement which recurs three times, identify also what happens immediately *after* each statement. What occurs after that event or exchange in each case?

4. Look also at 10:46-52 and compare it with 8:22-26. Note at what point in each section both occur. Any significance? Who is seeing and following?

5. What is the meaning of 8:31-38? Notice the title "Son of man" in verses 31 and 38. What did we say about this title in chapter 2? What two concepts are associated with it here? Look again in Daniel 7:13, 14 and also Mark 9:31 and 10:33.

6. Read 9:30-41 and 10:32-45. How do these texts (segments?) compare with 8:31-38? Do you see the carefully designed pattern? How, specifically, is 10:45 related to 10:42-45? What is the relationship between Jesus and the disciple?

7. The term "Christology" is used to denote "who Jesus is." A study of Christology usually focuses on the meaning and origin of titles used to describe Jesus, such as "Messiah," "Son of man," and "Lord." What is the relationship between Christology and discipleship in this section of Mark?

EXPOSITION: Mark 8:27–10:52

"And Jesus went on with his disciples, to the village of Caesarea Philippi; and on the way he asked his disciples, 'Who do men say that I am?' And they told him, 'John the Baptist; and others say, Elijah; and others one of the prophets.' And he asked them, 'But who do you say that I am?' Peter asked him, 'You are the Christ.' And he charged them to tell no one about him" (8:27-30).

These verses are recognized as the center of the Gospel of Mark, the pivotal point. Everything moves toward this point, the moment of messianic disclosure. For the first time those who would be Jesus' followers grasp hold of the nugget of truth, a sequel to the feedings of the multitudes. Those feedings, intended to be signs of messianic disclosure, accomplished their purpose.

Recapitulate the sequence of events from 6:30 to 8:30 and ponder their significance. The key themes are bread and understanding with chapter seven showing two contrasting responses. Then after a double touch, the blind man sees and pronto, the Great Confession. Put it all together; hear and see for yourself. The secret is disclosed. There is nothing hid, except to be made manifest. The hidden is coming to light; the seed is bursting and beginning to sprout! Read 8:29 aloud. Stand up and read it again!

One might think that the Gospel should now end but we're really only at the midpoint. As soon as Peter announces Jesus as Messiah, Jesus begins to teach what messiahship means. But Peter was not ready for it; nor were the other disciples.

Let's look at 8:27 to 10:52 to observe their responses. Notice that this section of the Gospel begins and ends with a confession about Jesus. At the beginning Peter confesses Jesus as Messiah and at the end the blind man of Jericho cries out and acclaims Jesus as "Son of David." This section thus shows Jesus' kingly aspect from the viewpoint of those who acclaim him. He is king—Messiah! But Jesus immediately begins to present another view of messiahship.

He began to teach them, in 8:31, "that the Son of man must suffer many things, and be rejected by the elders and the chief priests and the scribes, and be killed, and after three days rise again." In this section of the Gospel, Mark takes greatest care in the arrangement of the truth that he wants to communicate because this truth is so precious and so central to the whole Gospel. Three times Jesus announces his coming passion, in 8:31, 9:31, and 10:33. Read each of these texts in your Bible.

The Disciples' Responses

Immediately after these three announcements of the passion, the text clearly indicates that in each case the disciples do not understand what Jesus was talking about. Look at what happens in 8:32. Peter tries to rebuke Jesus! Peter, rebuking Jesus?! Peter knows what messiahs should do. Messiahs rule! They don't die!

But Peter is wrong and Jesus severely rebukes him. Jesus turns to Peter and says, "What you are saying is of satanic origin. It is not of God. Get behind me." If you look back into chapter 3 to the controversy over Jesus' source of power—whether Jesus is doing his work by God's power or Satan's—you see again the clash in perceptions as to what constitutes God's work and way versus Satan's work and way. The disciples are on the wrong side of the issue. Jesus says that the way of suffering, the way of the cross, is the way of God for the Messiah!

Look now at what happens in 9:32 after the second announcement of Jesus' suffering. The disciples' response is almost humorous, but also sad. "They did not understand the saying, and they were afraid to ask him." Wouldn't you have been afraid to ask about its meaning if you had received such a sharp tongue-lashing on the first attempt? So, rather than risk another scolding or face up to the agony of the predicted events, the disciples indulge in thoughts of imminent political pomp and prestige. As they walk on the way, leading eventually to Jerusalem (ch. 11), they wonder, "Which one of us is going to be the greatest in the coming kingdom?" That is where *their* minds are; but Jesus' mind is fixed on the cross.

The same distance between Jesus and the disciples emerges again in the third cycle, in 10:32 ff. In verse 25, right after the third passion announcement, James and John, the sons of Zebedee, come forward to Jesus and want him to do whatever they ask him, specifically, to promise them top seats in the coming kingdom. "Grant us to sit, one at your right hand and one at your left, in your glory." The disciples, in effect, are thinking and saying, "When you get that kingdom established, that kingdom that you've talked about in the parables and that's going to engulf the world, and rule even over Rome, couldn't you somehow arrange it so that we'd get the left and right seats by your side?!" Or, to modernize it, "Please promise to appoint one of us as Secretary of State and the other as Secretary of Defense, or as vice-president, if you prefer!" Even after Peter's confession that Jesus is the Messiah, the disciples still do not understand.

Jesus Teaches Discipleship

Mark's careful structural design correlated with his ever so special emphasis continues. Next in each of these three cases Jesus teaches discipleship. In 8:34, "If any man would come after me, let him deny himself and take up his cross and follow me. . . . What does it profit a man, to gain the whole world and forfeit his life? For what can a man give in return for his life?" The answer to the disciples' grasp for political power is the way of the cross.

In the second cycle the teaching on discipleship begins in 9:35: "If any one would be first, he must be last of all and

servant of all. And he took a child, and put him in the midst
of them; and taking him in his arms, he said to them,
'Whoever receives one such child in my name receives me;
and whoever receives me, receives not me but him who sent
me.' " In this case the disciples are vying for prestige among
themselves, querying who is going to be the greatest. To correct them, Jesus takes a child into his arms and says they must
be ready to receive and serve the needs of such little ones. In
that society the child had no rights or power, no greatness.[1]
The call to serve those without status and rights, including
certainly the poor and handicapped today, is followed by
severest judgment upon those who cause such to sin (9:42). In
10:14-15, the child models the way into the kingdom, a way
where quests for greatness are bulls in china closets.

In the third round, in 10:38-45, Jesus points the disciples
to the role of the servant. In contrast to seeking for positions
of rule and fame, Jesus calls his disciples to the cup of suffering and death (compare 14:36). Jesus calls his followers to
nonconformity from worldly thinking: "You know that those
who are supposed to rule over the Gentiles lord it over them,
and their great men exercise authority over them. But it shall
not be so among you; but whoever would be great among you
must be your servant, and whoever would be first among you
must be slave of all. For the son of man also came not to be
served but to serve, and to give his life as a ransom for
many." Our call to be servants is rooted in what Jesus himself
did. He was servant supreme, even giving his life for others.
Verse 45 is rightly called the golden text of Mark's Gospel.

To summarize the three points above: Jesus' answer to
wanting to rule by *power* is the way of the cross and learning
what that means in life. His answer to grasping for *prestige* is
service to the child, one who has no status based on rights.
And the answer to quest for *position* is the role of the servant,
one who serves in humble ways and is willing to suffer and
even die for others.

In this section of Mark's Gospel, the central section, we have these three segments, each of which has three parts: passion prediction, failure to understand, and teaching on discipleship. The threefold structure of these three segments may be portrayed as follows:

Passion Announcement	Disciples Don't Understand	Teaching on Discipleship
8:31	8:32-33	8:34-38
9:31	9:32-34	9:35-41
10:32-34	10:35-41	10:38-45

In each cycle of interchange the disciples reflect worldly ways of thinking and Jesus' teaching presents the kingdom perspective. The contrast between the two can be clearly seen in a structural outline of the issues and answers in each case:

Disciples' Temptation	Jesus' Answer
To expect the Messiah to rule by *power* (8:32, 33)	The way of the cross (8:34-38)
To gain *prestige* in the messianic kingdom (9:32-34)	The model of the child (9:35-41)
To attain *positions* or privilege in the kingdom (10:35-37)	The role of the servant (10:38-45)

Look now at the structural diagram for this chapter. Note that it is not complete. The next chapter will focus on 9:1-29 and 9:42—10:31 and develop two more themes in this section related to discipleship.

The Messiah of the Cross

From the viewpoint of Jewish theology, this section of Mark's Gospel presents a fundamental contradiction. Once confessed as Messiah, Jesus says "it is necessary" for the Messiah to suffer and die. The term in the Greek text, *dei* in 8:31, conveys the notion of divine necessity. God's purpose for Jesus includes the cross, a cross that arises out of historical circumstances—Jesus' own conflict with the religious leaders and his stand against their use of the temple.[2]

It is difficult for us to grasp the significance of this point, partly because we've heard and said it so often that its power and radicalness have been diminished by our familiarity with the words. Also, it's easy for us to talk about costly discipleship as long as none of us faces the ultimate test of choosing between continued life and a faithful obedience which leads to a martyr's death. Perhaps the following comments will help us see how new and radical, and how costly Jesus' teaching really is:

1. The Old Testament messianic hope anticipated a Messiah who would execute judgment upon the nations (Psalm 110:6), mete out vengeance (Isaiah 61:2b), "break them with a rod of iron, and dash them in pieces like a potter's vessel" (Psalm 2:9). This imagery gave rise to an expected militant Messiah, one who would conquer and rule through political power. Hence we should not be too hard on Peter (Mark 8:32, 33), since Peter represented sound Jewish theology.

Furthermore, many of us Christians continue to reflect Peter's mentality. We look at the cross as a necessary temporary phase for us and for Jesus but still cling to a literal political fulfillment of the Christian hope. Sometimes we associate it with the Book of Revelation and fail to notice that even in Revelation all victory is won not by a rod of iron but by *the slain Lamb,* the central figure of the book.

The Messiah of the cross is always the Messiah of the cross. The novelty of Jesus' teaching is that the way of the cross, the slain Lamb, is the reign of a "rod of iron" (Revelation 19:15). The word, not military weapons, is the sharp two-edged sword that issues from his mouth (Revelation 1:16, 19:15).

What Jewish theology never conceived, Jesus did. He linked together the suffering servant of Isaiah 40—55 with the messianic mission. The Jewish viewpoint does not identify these; hence Christians are dealing with the central issue of difference when they seek to show that Jesus fulfills Isaiah 53. And even as Christians, do we know what we're talking about?[3]

2. To disassociate himself from the prevailing messianic expectations, Jesus refers to himself as the "Son of man." ("the Son of man must suffer . . ."). In chapter 2 we observed that this title in its Old Testament context (Daniel 7:13, 14) connotes regal power of transcendent, heavenly origin. Rule over kings and nations comes not by the political messianic route but by God's divinely appointed means, the humiliation of the cross. He who ascends, ruling from the clouds of heaven, must first descend, experiencing suffering, death, and hades and he who has descended is he who has ascended far above the heavens (Ephesians 4:9, 10; compare John 1:51).

As used by Jesus—the Messiah of the cross—the term Son of man binds together tightly identification with mankind in suffering and death with heavenly rule and exaltation. The title signifies a conquest and reign that does not originate from the politics and power of this world. By identifying Jesus as Son of man, the messianic understanding of Jesus is linked firmly to a glory rooted in cross and suffering.

3. Roy Harrisville in his book, *The Miracle of Mark,*[4] has convincingly proposed that Mark's Gospel may be understood as a sermon proclaiming Jesus' life from the theological viewpoint of Philippians 2:5-11. Read this text and note its emphasis on Jesus' emptying himself, becoming a servant, and being obedient unto death. Jesus' exaltation is rooted, therefore, in his complete obedience and suffering servanthood.

As we will see in chapter 10 of this book, Mark discloses the confession of Jesus' divinity in the context of the cross and Jesus' death (15:37-39). Likewise, Mark shows that the heavenly voice which declares Jesus' divinity to three of the disciples (9:7) must be firmly linked to the suffering of the Son of man (9:12).

4. Jesus' life of obedience and service, even unto death, functions as the model for us as his followers. Read Mark 10:42-45 and note the word "for" which begins verse 45. The reason we should refuse to lord it over others, and live instead as servants of God and humanity, is *because* Jesus himself lived and died that way.

At the end of verse 45 the preposition, "for" (*anti*), "for many" carries not the notion of substitution, but the idea of "face to face," that is, his life, given as ransom, is a model for our lives.[5] Or put conversely, our lives of servanthood are to match his. *He is the prototype of what we are to be.*

5. Mark wrote his Gospel for Christians who were facing the threat and experience of martyrdom. Under Nero, in the late sixties AD, persons who identified themselves as Christians became vulnerable to death. Jesus' call in Mark's Gospel to take up the cross meant exactly what it says. Just as Jesus was crucified as a political rebel, so Christians were now regarded as deviants from and as threats to the political law and order of the Roman empire. For them, Jesus, not Caesar, was Lord. Such persons Caesar often killed.

Mark's teaching on discipleship, therefore, was not simply an interesting theological contribution nor a beautiful homiletical writing, but a practical exhortation to keep the faith: ". . . whoever loses his life for my sake and the gospel's will save it" (8:35b).

To follow Jesus, the Messiah of the cross, means to risk martyrdom. Christology—who Jesus is—and discipleship are firmly connected, united in the cross.

Lord,
    we identify with the blind men,
    and the blind, slow-to-learn disciples.
We too struggle and grapple
    with your call to take up Jesus' cross,
        to become as a child,
        to become servant of all.
Lord, our record and testimony isn't all that great,
    so we need your help
        to gain clear vision,
        to say no to worldly desires,
        to lose our lives for Jesus and the gospel.
We thank You for those times when You
    empowered us to make the right decisions, and
    enabled us to refuse easy responses
        to the temptations of imperious
            power, prestige, and position.
Help us to be faithful.
                    Amen.

STRUCTURAL DIAGRAM: 8:27—10:52

THE WAY OF THE CROSS TO THE KINGDOM OF GOD

You Are the Messiah	Passion Cycle 1		Passion Cycle 2			Passion Cycle 3		Blind Man	
8:27-30	8:31	8:38	9:1	9:29	9:30	9:41	9:42	10:31	10:32	10:45	10:46	10:52

Peter's Confession

Confession and Sight

Key Themes

Passion Announcement
___8:31___ ___9:31___ ___10:32-34___

Disciples Don't Understand
___8:32, 33___ ___9:32-34___ ___10:35-37___

Teaching on Discipleship
___8:34-37___ ___9:35-41___ ___10:38-45___

Reflection, Discussion, and Action

1. Reflect upon the crucial, central significance of Jesus' teaching on discipleship—its relation to Jesus' own person and mission (8:31; 10:45) and its function as a requirement for entering the kingdom of God.

2. Harold S. Bender in his booklet, *The Anabaptist Vision* (Herald Press, 1944), holds that the Anabaptist Reformation of the sixteenth century understood Christianity basically as discipleship (*Nachfolge*). Being a Christian means being a disciple, following and obeying. Do you agree? How does this emphasis match with what we've learned in this section of Mark's Gospel?

3. Notice again the firm connection between 10:42-44 and 10:45. Are you taking seriously the model of Jesus as servant for your own life?

4. This study sharply rebukes persons who aspire for political power, prestige, or position. But are all aspirations to power wrong? Is there any one of us who does not exert power in one form or another, or enjoy some prestige, or hold some position? Or consider Jesus himself who now holds power over all, including thrones and kingdoms (Colossians 1:15-20; 2:10; Ephesians 1:18-21) and has a name above every name (Philippians 2:10, 11). How do we bring these two realities together: servanthood and power? Read Philippians 2:5-11.

5. Examine your life's priorities. What specific changes can you make that will help you to become a more faithful disciple? Perhaps some changes require the support of a group of disciples. Is your study group or congregation able to give you the help you need? Perhaps one person's need and another's help can complement each other.

6. For practical suggestions in conforming your life to Jesus' call, see chapters 6 and 7 in Ronald J. Sider's book, *Rich Christians in an Age of Hunger* (Inter-Varsity, 1977).

7. Between now and your next study you may wish to read

Bender's and Sider's books mentioned above as well as Dietrich Bonhoeffer's *The Cost of Discipleship* (New York: Macmillan, 1962) and chapter 7, "The Disciple of Christ and the Way of the Cross," in John Howard Yoder's *The Politics of Jesus* (Grand Rapids: Eerdmans, 1972), pp. 115-134. Four different members could each read one book and report briefly to the group in the next session.

To Serve Is the Only Way

CHORIC
...the kingdom of God
is here
now
believe the good news
       repent
       turn around
       stand on your head—
                    the
                    "upside-down way
                    of seeing things"
                    has arrived!
Do you want to be first?
          —then be last;
          be servant of all!
          Do you want to live?
             —then die;
             stop living for yourself!
                 What shall a man do to die?
                 —just live for himself.
What shall a man do to live?
          —pronounce the death sentence
          on his desire to be
          for himself!
                  —not death to
                          the possible self;
                  —not death to
                          becoming that
                          which God intended;
                  —not death to
                          the self of worth
                          growing
                          into his likeness!

but DEATH to that desire
  to live
  only for oneself
      —instead of
      for others—
DEATH to that desire
  to grasp
  and cling to
  all that one is and has!

What does a man gain
  even
  if he wins the whole world
  at the cost of discovering his true self?
  Anyone who wishes to be a follower of mine
    must leave the grasping self behind
    must be willing to suffer and die
    must come with me:
  . . .whoever clings to his life
  will lose it
  But anyone who lets go,
  who pries loose
  his selfish grasp on things he calls his own
  so my kingdom can grow;
     that one will discover
     what it means to live,
     to be fully alive
      the
      "upside-down way
      of seeing things"
      has arrived!
    believe the good news
the kingdom of God
is here
now
  —the kingdom
  is
  where Jesus is
     —among Jew or Gentile
     bond or free
     male or female;

—the kingdom
is
wherever people walk the Jesus way
—from every nation
east and west
north and south;
—anyone—
anyone
who chooses
may come with me
may be a follower of mine...
—whether young or old
black or white
primitive
or cultured
anyone
who wishes to be
a follower of mine...
...must come
with me

(must
come
with me)

The Son of Man himself
did not come to be served
but to serve
and to give his life
to set many others free.
the servant died
on the way
to exaltation

—From *To Walk in the Way*

Chapter 8

Jesus' Way to the Kingdom of God

(Mark 8:27—10:52)

Presession Study

1. By now you may have discovered a thematic unity to this section, but 9:1-29 and 9:42—10:31 do not easily fit into the emphases of the rest of the section. Or do they? One term recurs quite often in these two passages, especially in 10:13-31. What is it?

2. Read the entire section again; observe *where* it all takes place. After locating towns and cities, look again, and again, until you find it. Look closely at 8:27 and 10:52, the first and last verses of the section. Where does each occur? Just as 6:30—8:21 has its two main events set in the wilderness, so these events happen in (on) _____.

3. By now the three main emphases of the section may have surfaced in your mind. The section teaches _____ which leads one _____ to the _____.

4. What does 9:1 mean? Is there any relationship between this verse and what immediately follows? Further,

how does the transfiguration relate to Peter's great confession? Is there any relationship between 9:1, the transfiguration, and Jesus' healing of the epileptic boy in 9:14-29?

5. Read carefully 9:9-13. Notice how these verses bring together several major themes of Mark's Gospel. What are they?

6. How do Jesus' teachings against divorce and riches fit into the emphases of the section? Notice the similarity between the questions of verses 2 and 17. What does this say about the questioners' mind-set? In contrast to this, feel the impact of verses 15 and 27.

7. As you reflect upon the entire teaching of this section, ponder the significance of the title of Guy Hershberger's book, *The Way of the Cross in Human Relations* (Herald Press, 1958).

EXPOSITION: MARK 8:27–10:52

The exposition of this chapter focuses first on two segments in this central, crucial section of the Gospel (9:1-29 and 9:42—10:31). Second, it considers the geographical-theological setting of this section. What we learn from these two aspects of study will contribute further to this section's teaching on discipleship.

In our last study we observed Mark's triple threefold presentation of Jesus' passion prediction, the disciples' failure to understand, and Jesus' subsequent teaching on discipleship. Placed between these three cycles of teaching on discipleship are supplemental teaching, instruction, and challenge regarding the kingdom of God.

Segment 9:1-29

Look in 9:1. "Truly, I say to you, there are some standing here who will not taste death before they see that the kingdom of God has come with power." What does that refer to? Some say the resurrection; some, the second coming; some, Pentecost; and some, on the basis of what follows in verses 2-9, the transfiguration.

I don't think it's necessary to choose sharply between these answers, but I do think that the transfiguration should receive immediate and careful consideration. When Jesus is transfigured on the mountain before three of his disciples and the voice comes from heaven, "This is my beloved Son; listen to him," we preview the kingdom power. We get a glimpse of the power accompanying his resurrection from the dead (Romans 1:4). Notice that in both Mark 9:7 and Romans 1:4 Jesus is designated "Son (of God)" in the context of and on the basis of his resurrection (transfiguration) power. Jesus' resurrection makes all the difference in and for the world.

After Jesus and "the inner three" come down from the mountain, they find the other disciples trying to cast out an evil spirit and, as with Moses of old, the initial statement is, "O faithless generation, how long am I to bear with you?" (v. 19). Later in the story Jesus takes the boy by the hand and lifts him up. Then in verse 27, it says, "he arose," the same word used to announce Jesus' own resurrection at the end of each passion prediction (8:31, 9:31, 10:34) and also in 9:10. This segment then, from 9:1-29, may be regarded as a preview of the kingdom power, not the kind of power the disciples expected, but a power that overcomes death itself.

But the preview of the resurrection power is not gospel unless toned by the reality of the cross. Verses 9-13 set the vision of power within the prior event of suffering, both for Jesus and John the Baptist, the Elijah who has come "first to restore all things." This double advent of Elijah and the Messiah, John and Jesus, sets God's restoration calendar into eleventh hour motion. Note the same sequence in the Gospel's prologue: first John appears (*egeneto,* 1:4) and then Jesus appears (*egeneto,* 1:9). God's new age has dawned. His purposes are being fulfilled.

Notice especially verse 9. This is the *last* command to secrecy. With it is a time condition—keep this secret "until the Son of man . . . [has] risen from the dead." After the resurrection the truth of Jesus' identity and person can be understood for what it is. But how is "rising from the dead" related to political messianic rule (verse 10)? The disciples couldn't put it together! All they knew was Jewish theology; Christian theology had not yet been born.

Segment 9:42—10:31

In 9:42—10:31, the segment between the second and third cycles on discipleship, Jesus teaches the cost of entering the kingdom of God. At the end of chapter 9 Jesus says that if your eye offends you, you should pluck it out in order that you don't miss the kingdom of God.

Next comes the discussion on divorce, initiated by the

Pharisees. Jesus' response points to the sanctity of marriage, the ethic of the kingdom. Jesus transcends the legal manipulative attitude of the Pharisees and declares the divine will.

In verses 13-15, the child again becomes the model, this time as the model of one who enters the kingdom through no merit of self or law-keeping.

Then follows the story of the rich man who comes and meets Jesus in the way, asking what he must do to inherit eternal life. The kingdom is entered not simply by managing to keep a good record (10:2 and 17-20) but by doing the will of God (10:6-9, 21, 22). Covenant faithfulness, both in marriage and sharing wealth with the poor, represents God's will and kingdom ethics. Verses 23-31 then underscore how hard it is for wealthy people, those who have status and power, to make it into the kingdom. But with God it is possible (v. 27), meaning that God's power enables us to pay the cost of discipleship and enter the kingdom of God. Whatever disciples pay to follow Jesus will not go unrewarded (10:28-30).

The Kingdom of God

A key phrase in both 9:1-29 and 9:42—10:31 is "kingdom of God." It appears in 9:1, 47; 10:14, 15, 23, 24, 25. In 9:47 and 10:23-25 the longer phrase, "to enter the kingdom of God," occurs. This phrase in the Greek text is identical to the phrase in Deuteronomy (in the Greek Septuagint translation of the Old Testament) which describes Israel's entrance into the land of Canaan.[1]

This similarity and others have led to the observation that Mark 8:27—10:52 uses much imagery from Exodus. Israel's "entering into the land" (Deuteronomy 1:8; 4:1; 6:18; 16:20) is transposed into the disciples' "entering the kingdom of God." Both Moses and Jesus descend from the mountain to encounter the unbelief of the people (Mark 9:19).

Numerous parallel themes occur also in the transfiguration: Jesus and Moses take *three* persons up on the *mountain*

(Mark 9:2; Exodus 24:1, 9, 12, 15) after *six* days (Mark 9:7; Exodus 24:16); the countenances glisten (Mark 9:2, 3; Exodus 34:29-35), and a voice comes from the cloud on the seventh day (Mark 9:2, 7; Exodus 24:16). And in both instances they discuss the building of tents or a tabernacle (Mark 9:5; Exodus 25:9).

One might also note that in both narratives, while they are beyond the Jordan about to cross over to enter the land (Mark 10:1), they discuss the issue of divorce (Mark 10:2-12; Deuteronomy 24). Further, in both cases, after crossing the Jordan, they come to Jericho, which Mark mentions twice (10:46, Joshua 4:19; 5:13; 6:1). Werner Kelber, a scholar who has done extensive study of Mark's Gospel, has also pointed out that Mark frequently uses the Old Testament exodus and entrance vocabulary. He uses in a redactional way "go out" or "depart" (*exerchesthai*) nineteen times and "to come in" or "enter" (*eiserchesthai*) eighteen times.[2] Kelber suggests that

> . . . the Markan entrance formula is ultimately derived from a translation of Deuteronomy's entrance tradition into an eschatological key. Modeled after Israel's first entrance, the present journey into the kingdom constitutes a second entry into the promised land.[3]

Further, one might note that, while in Israel's experience only a few would live to see the promised land, in Mark 9:1 "some standing here . . . will not taste death before they see that the kingdom of God has come with power."[4]

Christology—who is Jesus; discipleship—follow me (cross, child, and servant); and kingdom of God—the Messiah's destiny for the disciple—these are the leading emphases of this crucial section, the heart of the Gospel of Mark. The promise of the land has become the promise of the kingdom of God. The "meek . . . shall inherit the earth" (Matthew 5:5). The descendants of Abraham shall "inherit the world" (Romans 4:13).

Where Did It All Happen?

These observations provide the background to appreciate another insight. In the presession study questions, I asked you where all these events took place. In Caesarea Philippi (8:27)? In Capernaum (9:33)? In Judea (10:1)? In the house (10:10)? Yes, yes, but . . . behind these occasional places another term occurs, the little word, "way." Not all translations read "way" in all cases; sometimes it's translated "road" or "journey." But in the Greek text, it's always the same word, *hodos,* the normal word for "way." Look in 8:27; 9:33, 34; 10:17, 32, 46, 52. Note especially how the phrase occurs in the first verse and last verse of the section. Further, it is the very last phrase (*en tē hodō*) of the entire section. Just as the first blind man's receiving sight symbolized the breakthrough of spiritual sight which the disciples received (8:22-29), so the receiving of sight by this second blind man, Bartimaeus, who was sitting *beside the way,* symbolizes what's happening to the disciples. They follow Jesus *on the way* of *discipleship* that leads to the *kingdom of God.*

Look now at the structural summary at the end of this exposition.

This is why Mark's Gospel is called the Gospel of the Way. Look also at Mark 1:2, 3. Mark alone connects two texts from the Old Testament prophets that bear witness to this message of the way, the one from Malachi, "Behold, I send my messenger before thy face, who shall prepare thy way," and the other from Isaiah 40:3, "The voice of one crying in the wilderness: Prepare the way of the Lord, make his paths straight."

This "way of the Lord," the way of the Messiah, calls us to discipleship that leads to the kingdom of God. The question confronts *us,* Are *we* walking in *this way* which leads us to God's kingdom? Where are we *on the way*—refusing imperious power and following the way of the cross? Saying no to prestige and modeling a child's status? Rejecting concern

about position and willingly becoming servants, who live to
serve and give, for others?

> *O Lord God,*
> *in Jesus, our Savior and Leader,*
> *You have called us to your kingdom,*
> *You have shown us the way to the kingdom.*
> *Help us see ourselves*
> *as we really are.*
> *We want to be your followers,*
> *but what have we been talking about*
> *on the way?*
> *How often do we talk about*
> *the kingdom,*
> *or*
> *who is the greatest,*
> *what positions we hold,*
> *what we hope to achieve?*
> *Touch our eyes and our hearts*
> *so that we may see,*
> *believe, and*
> *follow*
> *the way of the cross*
> *to the kingdom of God.*
> *Through Jesus our Lord.*
>
> *Amen.*

STRUCTURAL DIAGRAM: 8:27—10:52

THE WAY OF THE CROSS TO THE KINGDOM OF GOD

You Are the Messiah	Passion Cycle 1	Preview of Kingdom Power	Passion Cycle 2	The Cost of the Kingdom	Passion Cycle 3	Blind Man
8:27-30	8:31 8:38	9:1 9:29	9:30 9:41	9:42	10:31 10:32 10:45	10:46 10:52

Peter's Confession

Confession and Sight

Key Themes

Passion Announcement
8:31 ———— 9:31 ———— 10:32-34

Disciples Don't Understand
8:32, 33 ———— 9:32-34 ———— 10:35-37

Teaching on Discipleship
8:34-37 ———— 9:35-41 ———— 10:38-45

Kingdom of God
9:1 ———— 9:47; 10:14, 15, 23, 24, 25

The Way (*Hodos*)
8:27 ———— 9:33,34 ———— 10:17 ———— 10:32 ———— 10:46 ———— 10:52

Reflection, Discussion, and Action

1. Reflect upon the crucial, central significance of Jesus' teaching on discipleship—its relation to Jesus' own person and mission (8:31; 10:45) and its function as a requirement for entering the kingdom of God.

2. What is the significance of 10:15 and 27, especially as these verses present a contrast to verses 2 and 17? Alvin Beachy's doctoral study, now published under the title, *The Concept of Grace in the Radical Reformation* (E. de Graaf, 1977), shows that the Anabaptist view of discipleship was also rooted in grace. God's grace enables obedience. What does it mean to talk about "discipleship in (by, under) grace"? What light does such emphasis shed upon the church's position on divorce? On persons who are divorced and remarried? On persons with wealth?

3. Discuss this statement: God's grace and forgiveness may never become an excuse for us to relax in our obedience and discipleship; but no disciple, however faithful he may be, can live without grace, both to empower and to forgive.

4. Jesus' teaching against divorce hits us hard as Christians in two ways: (1) divorces are happening among Christians but Jesus teaches that divorce is wrong; it is not what God intends, and (2) while the Pharisees had set rules which had the effect of making divorce morally acceptable in certain cases, Jesus does not support such a legalistic approach—and we too are tempted to find a legal way to *approve* it in *some* instances. Discuss how your congregation can hold to the divine will and at the same time accept and forgive the one who sins in this regard.

5. Three points are helpful in enabling us to understand the relationship between divorce and remarriage:

(1) *"What* God joins. . . ." The marriage bond itself is sacred and should not be broken.

(2) As Mark 10:11 indicates, divorce and remarriage went together. It was assumed in the Jewish culture (partly

for economic reasons) that a divorced person would remarry.
(3) The term "commit adultery" is one word, a verb, in
Greek and is best translated "to adulterate," which means to
weaken or dilute. What is adulterated? The first marriage
bond! The sin and failure is in relationship to the former marriage failure. Remarriage, while not the sin itself, finalizes the
sin of the former failure in covenant promise.

How can you and your congregation help marriages to
remain strong so that they are not adulterated through lust,
conflict, separation, divorce, and remarriage?

6. Both riches and adulterated marriages are present-
day threats to obedient discipleship that leads to the kingdom
of God. In the same way that your congregation assists marriages to become sacred relationships, can your congregation
help its members to keep riches in proper perspective (10:17-
25)?

7. Does this study help you understand why the first
(Christian) believers were called "those of the Way" (Acts
9:2; 22:4; 24:14, 22)? And does it help you understand part of
the title of this book?

A Hard Choice

CHORIC

. . . that is why
those who cling to
    things
              or
    dogma
              or
    power
              or
    fame
              or
    security
have difficulty
        entering
        the kingdom of God
. . . it's a hard choice.

—From *To Walk in the Way*

Part III

THE TEMPLE
FOR ALL NATIONS

"Is it not written,
'My house
shall be called a house of prayer
for all the nations'?"

Chapter 9

Jesus: Judge of Exclusivism

(Mark 11—13)

Presession Study

1. Read these three chapters twice, first quickly and then more slowly. What mood do they create? With whom do you identify in these chapters? Who are Jesus' opponents?

2. Let us assume that each chapter in this section is a separate segment (review again the terms "section" and "segment" in Appendix II, Section B). What descriptive titles would you give each segment? Does 12:1-12 fit better with chapter 11 or chapter 12?

3. If finding segment titles is difficult, take time to give each paragraph a descriptive title. Notice the "sandwiching" in 11:12-22. Is there any significance to this? How might Jeremiah 24 assist us in understanding Mark's symbolism in the sandwiching?

4. Notice what is said in 11:10 and compare this to Bartimaeus' acclamation in 10:47, 48. What view of Jesus do the common people reflect?

5. Of what does Jesus "cleanse" the temple? In what

part of the temple did the cleansing occur? Any significance?
Note the last part of Mark's quotation from Isaiah. Note the
Old Testament context of these quotations, Isaiah 56 and
Jeremiah 7.

6. How does 11:27-33 relate to what precedes it in the
chapter? Where does this event occur (verse 27)?

7. Are there levels of allegory in the parable of the
wicked tenants? That is, who or what might the tenants
represent? The vineyard (see Isaiah 5)? The tower? The
servants? The son?

8. In chapter 12, verse 12, to whom does the word
"they" refer?

9. How does Jesus answer each of the questions in
12:13-34? What is the significance of his counter-question in
verses 35-37? How do verses 38-44 carry forward the theme of
the chapter?

10. What is chapter 13 speaking about? Notice the "subject" in verses 1-4. Are we talking about the same thing as we
did in chapters 11 and 12? If so, *what* is it? How is 13:10 related to 11:17? What is the meaning of verse 14? Note the difficulty of verse 30. What is the punch line of the chapter
(verses 32-37)?

11. Do you notice a continuous theme in all three
chapters—something similar to "the way" *(hodos)* in 8:27—
10:52?

12. Now rethink question 2. What titles would you give
each chapter?

EXPOSITION: MARK 11–13

They arrived at Jericho (10:46). Until then the disciples had not understood Jesus. Like blind Bartimaeus, they needed sight—spiritual sight to perceive Jesus' destiny in Jerusalem. The eyes of Bartimaeus were opened, and he followed Jesus *also*—even to Jerusalem (recall 10:32). Whether the disciples fully understand even at this time remains doubtful.

Once in Jerusalem, the mood shifts from teaching to action. The disciples drop backstage in these chapters, securing a donkey (11:1 ff.), inquiring about the withered fig tree (11:21), and framing the Olivet discourse with comment and question (13:1-4). The action, however, is between Jesus and the temple, *the* institution most precious to the religious leaders. Mark, in fact, makes the point that Jesus' Palm Sunday entry climaxed with Jesus' going into the temple, looking it over, and then going out for the night.[1]

Jesus' entry into Jerusalem echoes the combined themes of the baptismal voice (kingship and servanthood). Jesus chooses a colt on which to ride, symbolic of humility. But he is acclaimed for kingly messianic destiny (11:10). The crowds expect him to establish "the kingdom of our father David!" One can only imagine what awe, hope, and silence fell upon the crowd as Jesus entered the temple. The king comes into the "temple of the kingdom!"[2]

But now the mood of the text changes; it is no longer set by the crowd, but by Jesus. Jesus returns on Monday morning not to establish a regal throne in the temple of the kingdom but to demonstrate that his kingship transcends the temple. Not only is he lord of the sabbath (2:28), but he is also lord of the temple!

Several points merit notice. The "cleansing" or better, "demonstration," occurred in the court of the Gentiles where the money-changers had set up their seats for commerce. The text specifically mentions "those who sold pigeons," the offering bought by the poor. The sellers not only ripped off the poor by gross overcharges, but also encroached upon the rights and space of the Gentiles to worship God. If you want to see Jesus go into action, just cheat the poor and squeeze out the Gentiles! Notice, he not only overturned the tables (quite a demonstration!), but he also "would not allow anyone to carry anything through the temple," meaning the Gentile court, in which the cleansing occurred. Jesus set new rules for the temple, just as he did for the sabbath. Taking on two of the most sacred institutions, Jesus was indeed revolutionary!

Mark sees the significance of the event also from his later church stance in which Gentiles had come to be accepted into the church, but not without much trauma (Acts 15, Galatians 3-4, Romans 4). In the quotation from Isaiah 56:7—a vision of the ingathering of foreigners and outcasts—Mark alone of the Gospel writers includes the final phrase "for all the nations." Mark emphasizes that the cleansing is for the sake of the nations, but "you have made it a den of robbers." Robbers were using the temple for a den, their hideout headquarters! This quotation, strikingly enough, comes from Jeremiah 7 (verse 11), Jeremiah's temple court sermon in which he announces the certain doom and destruction of Jerusalem.

Lest the point of Jesus' prophetic act be missed, Mark sandwiches the story between the cursing, withering, and death of the fig tree. The point of the fig tree account is not Jesus' vendetta against fig trees, fruit or no fruit, out of season or in, but that the doom and destiny of the fig tree casts its shadow over the temple.

Then follows in tense, cryptic comment the portent of "this mountain" on which the temple stood being cast into the sea (verse 23). But the life of faith and its true piety in prayer (verse 24), and forgiveness (verse 25), survive, and flourish in liberation from the temple institution.

Is it any wonder that Jesus is now questioned about his authority (verses 27-33) "as he was walking in the temple" (verse 27)?! Jesus, however, does not answer directly, but rather demands an answer. Jesus is not in a corner; rather the "chief priests and the scribes and the elders" and the whole world are in a corner!

Chapter 11 is aptly titled *Jesus Comes to, Cleanses, and Claims the Temple.*

At this point I must tell you a dream. About seven years ago when I was working hard on this part of Mark's Gospel, doing my doctoral dissertation at Princeton Theological Seminary, I dreamed on a Saturday night that I had been asked by my bishop father-in-law to preach the next morning at Plains Mennonite Church. I accepted and (oh, how vivid the dream) when I got up to speak, I found myself in a dreadful situation, the "abomination of desolation." In this historic peace church, the pulpit had been moved to the left and a huge United States flag was erected just right of center.

I stood at the pulpit, but the prepared sermon had completely left me. I stood in silence, looking full-eyed at the congregation for what seemed to be several minutes. I then went over to the flag, knocked it down from the platform over the railing, and then went back to the pulpit. After a moment of breathless silence, I spoke; "This house shall be a house of prayer *for all nations,* but you have made it a den of Americanism." I sat down. The sermon was ended. I awoke trembling and could not sleep. God had spoken.

The Temple Tenants

In chapter 12, the temple tenants fall under the deftly struck sword of Jesus' words. The parable against the wicked tenants carries allegorical overtones, as evidenced by verse 12, "for they perceived that he had told the parable against them." Who is the "they" and "them"? The immediate context of the parable suggests that "they" refers to the "tenants" of the parable. However, the actual referent is likely "the chief priests and the scribes and the elders" of 11:27 and the "they" of 12:13, who are represented in turn by the Pharisees and Herodians (verse 13), the Sadducees (verse 18), and one of the scribes (verse 28). We cannot avoid the conclusion that the wicked tenants of the parable are indeed the religious leaders who killed not only the servants and the prophets, but will also kill the son (Son), Jesus.

As numerous commentators suggest, the vineyard probably symbolizes Israel itself (as in Isaiah 5) or even Jerusalem, the religious and political center of Israel. The hedge (the wall) and the tower (the temple) are allegorical allusions shining through the parable. The destiny of the tenants and the destiny of the stone, Jesus, are clearly forecast in verses 9-10. Matthew goes a step further and forecasts also the destiny of the vineyard (Matthew 21:43)! Did you know that verse was in your Bible?

Verses 13-34 describe for us what Paul Minear has aptly entitled "Traps Set for the Son."[3] But in the final analysis, the questioners, not Jesus, are those trapped. Notice that after a long vacation or research assignment some of the Pharisees in cahoots with some of the Herodians (a most unlikely political coalition) now return with the perfect plan "to entrap" (12:13) and "destroy him" (3:6). Listen to their sinister sarcasm and ironic quest for truth. "Teacher, we know that you are true, and care for no man; for you do not regard the position of men [how well they had discovered!], but truly teach the way of God. Is it lawful to pay taxes to Caesar, or not? Should we pay them, or should we not?"

The tax issue in first-century Palestine was explosive. The Zealots, revolutionaries against Rome, refused payment; the Sadducees, and certainly the Herodians, who collaborated with Rome, paid taxes in good conscience; the Pharisees, having internalized and legalized their piety, paid, but with anguish. By comparing this trap with the following one and the conflict stories of 2:1—3:6, it is safe to say that the Pharisees and Herodians considered Jesus to be "on the other side of the issue." They held him to be a tax refuser (see Luke 23:2). The trap was set.

For Jesus to say no to the payment of taxes would have publicly exposed him as an insurrectionist, giving the Romans an excuse to rid the land of him. By saying, "Yes, pay taxes," Jesus would have settled with the same compromise as that of the Herodians and Pharisees, an unlikely position for Jesus.

Jesus, the Son, snaps the trap on their own toes. He asks for a denarius, the prescribed tax coin, on which appeared the emperor's claim to deity.[4] Zealots wouldn't touch the coin and Jesus had none. Producing the coin was itself an act of self-judgment, and a judgment upon all who carried it. Jesus' word-sword then pierced to the heart: "Render to Caesar the things that are Caesar's, and to God the things that are God's." No toe was not pinched. All were amazed at the wisdom of the answer and certainly the religious leaders were smitten with the agony of their own dilemma: for what does belong to Caesar and what does indeed belong to God?

Pharisees and Herodians down, next come the Sadducees. Using the Jewish practice of the levirate (in which a man's brother is obligated to marry a widowed wife), they seek to reduce the Pharisees' (and Jesus') belief in the resurrection to the level of the ludicrous. But Jesus, transcending their Sadducean mentality, says in effect that they know nothing of the kingdom reality which both transcends marriage and is promised by a God who is God of the living, and not of the dead.

Then comes one of the scribes, who, upon noting Jesus' wisdom, seeks to get his hermeneutical question answered: Which commandment is the greatest or most important? For first-century Jews, keeping the sabbath was most sacrosanct; but Jesus wouldn't say that, for it was certainly not his position. Again, Jesus transcends scribal mentality and sums up the whole law in the command of love for God and neighbor.

After this short inning of three up and three down, Jesus hits a home run (verses 35-37). How can you scribes say that the Messiah (Christ) must be the *son* of David when David himself calls him *his Lord*. In the temple (verse 35) he asks that question. There is no answer, only glad response from the crowds. After taking the offensive through this unanswered riddle, Jesus speaks with prophetic authority. First he denounces scribal piety (vv. 38-40). Then, in the story of the widow's mite he illustrates the nature of true piety (vv. 41-44).

Chapter 12 may be titled: *Temple Tenants Judged and Condemned.*

The Olivet Discourse

Chapter 13 then takes us across the Kidron Valley to the Mount of Olives for a discussion of the fate of the temple, glistening with splendor on opposite Mount Zion. The disciples are enthralled by its beauty, and admire its wonderful stones and architecture. In this setting Jesus announces the temple's destruction, its end. Shocked beyond words, only later do the four disciples (the ones called first—1:16-20) privately ask for more information. But I doubt that they really wanted to hear the bad news.

The Olivet discourse then describes the sign(s) that will precede and accompany the certain forthcoming destruction of the temple. The signs preceding the end are the rise of Messianic pretenders (verses 3-6); wars, earthquakes, famines (verses 7, 8); and persecution (verses 9-13). All this is common apocalyptic description of the crises of history, believed to precede the end. And for Mark, writing likely in the sixties, the end of the temple (AD 70) and the end of the age are not distinguished.[5] These points were common to Jewish and Christian descriptions of the end times as was the fear of the coming "desolating sacrilege," the "abomination of desolation" (verse 14).

Just as the Seleucid ruler, Antioches Epiphanes, had once desecrated the temple for three and one half years (168-165 BC), offering sacrifice to the pagan god Zeus (described in Daniel 11:31 ff. with the deliverance proclaimed in Daniel 12:7, after three and one-half years),[6] so the Jews feared the recurrence of "the abomination" as a portent of the end. In AD 40 it did almost happen[7] and as the tensions mounted in the mid-sixties with Nero's persecutions, the end appeared to be only around the corner. Note Mark's urgent parenthesis in verse 14: "(let the reader understand)." It may indeed be this word from Mark's Gospel, recalling and reaffirming the oracle of Jesus, that explains why Jewish Christians fled Jerusalem before its fall, taking refuge some fifty miles north within the secluded Transjordan town of Pella.[8] Josephus tells us about the indescribably horrible suffering, especially from the famine that accompanied those final days before the end (for example, a mother killing her nursing child and eating him for food).[9] Since Mark does not separate the end of the temple from the end of the age, but rather sees one portending the other, the coming of the Son of man for judgment follows immediately in verses 24-27.

Two exhortations conclude the discourse (verses 28-37). The first is a lesson from the fig tree. You know that when it puts forth leaves summer is near; so also you know that when these things take place, the coming of the Son of man is near. Verses 30-31 emphasize the certainty of the event. The final exhortation is to watchfulness and preparedness, the punch line for us as we live our Christian lives today.

But all of this misses one important point of the discourse and of Mark's Gospel. Verse 10 says, "And the gospel must first be preached to all nations." If on the one hand

Mark is concerned (1) to exhort Christians to faithful discipleship and (2) to prepare Christians for suffering and faithfulness in the end times, so also he is (3) equally concerned to call Christians to spread the gospel to all nations. The good news is for the whole world, and God is not finished until the Gentiles, the nations, hear the gospel.

This point will be extended in chapter 10. In this part of Mark's Gospel, the Gentile mission is set in the context of the doom upon and the end of Jewish exclusivism. The temple and its tenants are out of jobs.

Chapter 13 in the Gospel may be entitled *The End of the Temple.*

Before leaving this fateful picture, look carefully at the structural diagram summarizing this study.

Lord God,
  in the life of Jesus
    we have seen your love
      and felt your wrath.
We've learned that you won't tolerate
  oppressing the poor,
    infringing upon the rights of the outsiders, and
    making worship serve political ends.
Forgive us, O God,
  for our mixed up loyalties
  for our devotion to temples,
    vested interests, and
    the security of strict doctrinal positions.
Help us to be responsive to the needs of all people,
  to keep our doctrines subservient to your will, and
  to be prepared for the crisis of the end upon us.
Save us from your consuming judgment,
  for Jesus' sake.
                      Amen.

STRUCTURAL DIAGRAM OF CHAPTERS 11—13

JESUS AND THE TEMPLE

Jesus Comes to, Cleanses, and Claims the Temple	Jesus Judges and Condemns the Temple Tenants	Jesus Foretells the End of the Temple
11:1	11:33 | 12:1	12:44 | 13:1	13:37

Key Themes

temple (*hieron*)
11:11, 15, 15, 16 ———— 27 ———— (12:1-13) ———— 12:35 ———— 13:1, 3 ———— (13:14)
11:17   (the tenants)   (desecration)

all nations (*ethnē*)
11:17 ————————————————————— 13:10 ——————————
(Matthew 21:43)   (Luke 21:24)

Reflection, Action, and Discussion
1. Quite a bit of information on historical background is included in this chapter, especially in the footnotes. For more information in these areas, consult a Bible dictionary. (I recommend the *Interpreter's Dictionary of the Bible.*) Look up such terms as "Pella," "Antiochus Epiphanes," and "abomination of desolation." Chapter 2 of Donald Kraybill's recent book, *The Upside-Down Kingdom* (Herald Press, 1978), retells the history of the Jews' struggle to survive as a nation during the Maccabean period (after 165 BC) and Roman period (after 63 BC).

2. In many ways the break between this lesson and the next is only a "pause for station identification" since the themes are continued there and the issues resolved. But what do you think? Is Mark's final word actually no temple at all or is it a reclaiming and rebuilding of the temple?

3. What ways of thinking and acting in your own life and the life of your congregation fall under Jesus' sword of judgment against exclusivism? Are we guilty of keeping "the temple" to ourselves and encroaching upon the religious rights of others?

4. What is the point of the dream in this lesson? Occasionally one sees a Bible with a United States flag on its cover. What's the problem with mixing national allegiance with the Bible? What would Jesus say? What is the opposite of exclusivism? How do you feel about the sign one sometimes sees in public places: "No Shoes, No Shirt—No Service, No Exceptions"?

5. Payment of taxes used for harmful ends is as sticky a question now as it was in Jesus' time. Several years ago I wrote a paper on the "New Testament Teaching on the Payment of Taxes Used for War." You may get a copy from Mennonite Central Committee Peace Section, Akron, Pa. 17501, or from Mennonite Board of Congregational Ministries, Box 1245, Elkhart, Ind. 46515. See also my article, "A

New Testament Study on the Payment of War Taxes," *Sojourners* (Feb. 1979), pp. 18-21.

7. Have you and your congregation heeded the teaching of chapter 13? Are you willing to testify through suffering (vv. 9-13)? Are there areas in Christian discipleship where you compromise and withdraw rather than stand faithful, ready to take the consequences? Finally, are you ready for the final crisis and judgment (vv. 26-36)?

Chapter 10

Jesus: Messiah for the World

(Mark 14–16)

Presession Study

1. Read Mark, chapters 14 to 16. The last twelve verses of chapter 16 (vv. 9-20) are not to be regarded as part of the original Gospel's text (see footnote 11 of this chapter). It is commonly agreed by textual scholars that the Gospel either ends at verse 8 or that the original ending (the last wrap of the scroll) was mutilated and lost. Based on my understanding of the Gospel's emphases, as shown in this chapter and the next, I consider verse 8 to be the conclusion of the Gospel, even though its ending is oddly abrupt.

2. List key terms that recur in these chapters. Can you divide this section into segments? Where are the major breaks in thought, or beginnings of new stages in the passion event?

3. What portrait of Jesus emerges in these chapters? Which titles are applied to him?

4. Identify all the themes previously studied that are present in this final section. Describe how these reach their climax. What or where is the climax of the Gospel?

5. In 14:28 and 16:7 Mark stresses Jesus' resurrection appearance in Galilee. Look at Matthew 4:15 and note what Galilee symbolizes, in contrast to Jerusalem. In what way might these verses express both an important theme and part of the climax of Mark's Gospel?

6. What happens to the temple in this section? Is there any significance to the phrase "in three days" in 14:58?

7. Can you put the key themes together? Write an essay on how Mark 14—16 brings to a head the Gospel's purpose, themes, and emphases.

EXPOSITION: MARK 14–16

As you may have noticed, we never learn from Mark's Gospel the length of Jesus's ministry. Chapters 11—16, at least one third of the Gospel, focus on Jesus' last week in Jerusalem. But beyond that we get no idea how long Jesus spent in his public ministry.[1] In Mark we meet Jesus as an adult man (1:9). He begins his public work in Galilee (1:14 ff.), soon turns his back on the synagogue (3:6—7 ff.; except for Nazareth in 6:1-6), does his ministry by the sea, on the mountain, in the desert, and on the way. From 8:27, after arriving at Caesarea Philippi, to 10:52, the movement is generally toward Jerusalem.

Mark's Gospel has been called "a passion story with an extended introduction."[2] In 3:6 Pharisees and Herodians already plan Jesus' death. John's fate portends Jesus' future in that Jesus begins his ministry in the shadow of John's arrest (1:14, 15) and John's death is attached to Jesus' sending out of the twelve (6:7-29). Jesus not only calls his disciples to come *after him* and take up the *cross* (8:34), but the passion announcements anticipate the somber end (8:31; 9:31; 10:33). The servants of the vineyard kill the son (12:1-8) and a woman (Mary of Bethany according to John 12:1-8) anoints Jesus for his death. The cross casts its shadow over the entire Gospel.

From one point of view, Jesus' death is the result of his conflict with the religious leaders. They seek and plot to get rid of him (3:6, 12:13). Prophets who violate "holy" sabbath and temple traditions get killed.

From another point of view, though, the cross is a divine necessity: "the Son of man must suffer many things" (8:31; cf. 9:12).[3]

It would be wrong for us to disassociate these two points of view. Both are correct. God worked in and through the sin of humanity. The life of the incarnate Son exposed human sin for what it is—a clinging to security, even religious tradition, at the expense of receiving God's truth. The cross of Jesus receives a nail from each of us, hammered in by our "sabbaths" and our "temples."

Jesus' Death: Betrayed, But Prepared

Mark's Gospel shows Jesus' death as a *betrayal*. It is first a betrayal of Jesus by Judas (one of the twelve disciples) to the Jewish leaders (14:10, 11, 18, 21, 41, 42, 44). Second, it is a betrayal of Jesus by the Jews to the Romans (15:1, 10). And, third, it is a betrayal of Jesus by Pilate (the Romans) to death (15:15). The same Greek word (*paradidomi,* meaning "to deliver over" or "betray") is used in all ten instances. When disciples, Jews, and Romans are involved, what's the point of the question, Who crucified Jesus? Nevertheless, the question *is* asked; for centuries Christians have blamed Jews and Jews have blamed Christians.[4] But no one is guiltless (see Acts 4:27)!

Punctuating the first stage of Jesus' betrayal are (1) Jesus' making a covenant with his disciples in his death (vv. 17-25), (2) Jesus' own struggle with and acceptance of the cup of death in Gethsemane (vv. 32-42), and (3) Peter's threefold denial (vv. 30, 31, 66-72). We can readily identify with all three episodes. In the first we discover that our bond to Jesus or Jesus' bond to us is through his broken body and shed blood. We are covenant partners in and through the cross. In the second event, a portrait of agony, we identify both with Jesus in his struggle to accept death as the Father's will, and even more with the disciples who sleep while the Master suffers. In the third episode, we see ourselves again, pledging loyalty, but, when the chips are down, denying our connection to Jesus, saying "no" to the covenant-unto-death and spurning Jesus' agony of Gethsemane. No, Lord, we don't know who you are!

As R. H. Lightfoot has suggested,[5] the Olivet discourse's

threefold call to "watch" (13:33, 35, 37) already has its practical application in the passion narrative. The "master of the house" might come "in the evening, or at midnight, or at cockcrow, or in the morning" (13:35). And so:

> —at *evening* he comes and Judas' betrayal is announced (14:17, 18).
> —during the night, through the *midnight* hour, he comes three times to his inner three disciples and they are sleeping in Gethsemane (14:37-42).
> —at *cockcrow* Peter denies him three times (14:66-72).
> —and in the *morning,* the Jews deliver him to Pilate (15:1).

In the crisis of the cross, the judgment of the end has come upon us. "Watch therefore—for you do not know when. . . ."

It is also interesting to note a pattern of interchange in 14:1-25. Two types of preparation are going on. On one level, in verses 1, 2, 10, 11, 17-21 the Jewish leaders collaborate with Judas and plot Jesus' death. On another level, in 3-9, 12-16, 22-25, and 32-42, Jesus himself is prepared for and is preparing for his death. Mary anoints Jesus for his burial (3-9). The supper (12-16, 22-25) is the *last* supper: "I shall not drink again of the fruit of the vine until that day when I drink it new in the kingdom of God" (v. 25). And the covenant, his *last* will and testament (*diathēkē,* the word meaning testament or covenant), seals his relationship to his followers. Third, in Gethsemane (32-42) Jesus, even through agony, accepts his mission: ". . . remove this cup from me; yet not what I will, but what . . . [God] wilt" (v. 36). In this interchange God works out his mysterious purpose through interplay between evil conspiracy and the full obedience of the Son to the Father's will.

Look now at the structural diagram at the end of the exposition and grasp an overview of the section, noting especially the two levels of preparation for Jesus' death.

Mark's Leading Themes Reach Their Climax

Not only do Mark's emphases on the passion, cross, and watchful discipleship reach their climax in chapters 14—16, but his other themes such as the destiny of the temple, the identity of Jesus, and the Messiah for all nations also crescendo in these chapters. The specific charge used to open Jesus' mock trial (given by false witnesses) was: "We heard him say, 'I will destroy this temple that is made with hands, and in three days I will build another, not made with hands.' " Did Jesus say that? Did Jesus say he would destroy the temple? That issue is not a juvenile offense. Temple destroyers are traitors, rebels who get hanged or crucified.

Recall what we studied in chapters 11—13. The record appears to show Jesus as a revolutionary against the temple. Indeed, he did predict its destruction. But did he say, "*I* will destroy it"? John's Gospel preserves for us another account of what Jesus did say in this regard. Read John 2:19. It is not difficult to see how Jesus' angry opponents went from the statement in John 2:19 to the one in Mark 14:58. But what is the temple? What will be built again in three days? We know John's answer, yes, but we're studying Mark. What in Mark's Gospel will be rebuilt in three days? Mark's answer is substantially the same, but more subtly disclosed, as we will see.

But before we pursue that theme further, let us focus on the identity of Jesus in the passion story. Because Caiaphas, the high priest, could not get Jesus to answer the temple charge, he zeroed in on the "messianic inference" in the claim to rebuild the temple.[6] So he put the question to Jesus: "Are you the Messiah, the Son of the Blessed?" Only in Mark is Jesus' answer unequivocal, while Matthew and Luke record ambiguous answers.[7] Mark interprets the reply positively, repeating the stunning declaration of 6:50, *I AM (ego eimi),* thus bringing the high priest face-to-face with a divine epiphany. In this way Mark stresses the divine disclosure of Jesus, another surprise in the breaking of the secret. The words that follow, concurring with those of Matthew and Luke, are also astounding: "... and you will see the Son of man seated at the right hand of Power, and coming with the clouds of heaven." Recall the previous discussion of this title, "Son of man," a title designating transcendent sovereignty and ultimate power to judge and reign (Daniel 7:13, 14). In this appearance before Caiaphas, the charge against Jesus is two-edged—*destruction* of the temple in order that *he, the Messiah,* the Son of the Blessed, might rebuild it again. But how will such a charge be translated in a Roman court of law when the Jewish leaders deliver him over to the Romans?

Mark does not list the specific charges against Jesus as he is betrayed by the Jewish leaders to the Romans. Luke, however, does and they are: (1) national subversion, (2) teaching tax refusal, and (3) claiming to be Christ, a king. Pilate picks up this latter charge and, according to all the Gospels, focuses the question, "Are you the King of the Jews?" Imagine Pilate even dropping the words from his lips! Jesus' answer, "You have said so," amazingly puts the confession back on Pilate's lips so that the Roman procurator is left with the historical burden of having affirmed Jesus as King of the Jews (verse 9).   The point then becomes ironic when Pilate says (v. 12), "Then what shall I do with the man whom you [the Jewish crowd] call the King of the Jews?" Now *Pilate* certifies for the Jews the truth they deny. Finally, the inscription on the cross, "The King of the Jews" (15:26), reveals the truth—a truth denied by mass unbelief among the Jews (15:32), mocked by Roman complicity (15:18), but ironically, indirectly affirmed by both.

From the point of view held by Jesus, by Mark, and the followers of the Jesus Way (our view, too, I hope) it is important to note that these revelations of Jesus' identity—I Am, Son of man, and King of the Jews—are *all disclosed in the shadow of the cross.* That fits with the interconnection between 8:29 and 8:31. The secret may be revealed only when rightly understood: i.e., when the *Messiah dies,* obeys God's will unto death, even death on a cross. The King is Servant supreme.

For Mark this point of the temple's end, associated with two others, becomes the punch line, the climax of his Gospel. When Jesus breathed his last, Mark's first and only comments are:

1. The temple is done for, because of Jesus' death (15:38).
2. In his suffering and death Jesus is truly Son of God (15:39).
3. Not a Jew, but a Gentile perceives the full truth of God's secret (15:39).

The title, Son of God, may be understood in two ways, from both Jewish and Gentile uses of the term. From the Jewish Old Testament point of view it denotes one fully obedient to God and especially anointed by Him for service and salvation (see Exodus 4:22; Psalm 2:7; Isaiah 49:6). From the Hellenistic (Greek religious literature) point of view, it denotes one who possesses divine nature and superhuman powers. While Mark stresses the Jewish meaning, he does not disallow the Greek view. But the latter emphasis may be made only in the context of the former. That is the theology of Philippians 2:5-11, for which Mark's Gospel may be a theological commentary.[8] For Mark and Paul (as well as the other New Testament writers), Jesus' divine power is to be affirmed precisely in and through his obedience and suffering. In Jesus the divine and human are not contradictory but are harmoniously affirmed. In doing fully the will of his Father, even unto suffering and death, Jesus was fully (perfectly) human and fully (perfectly) divine.[9]

A suffering Messiah was so contrary to the Jewish expectations of the Messiah that Jesus' identity during his ministry was rightly enshrouded in secrecy. Mark intensifies this point by showing further that the Gentiles received what most Jews rejected. The Gospel's climax in 15:38, 39 shows this twofold response. The veil of the temple is torn in two and, immediately, a Gentile acclaims Jesus as Son of God.

Verse 38 is Mark's last word on the destiny of the temple. What does it mean? Was the curtain the one between the holy place and the holy of holies? Or was it the curtain at the front of the temple? While I think the former is more likely, the end result is the same. Mark is saying that the partitions which controlled hierarchical access into God's presence are done away with. The end of the temple's function has come! Now all people, including Gentiles, are invited to affirm Jesus and worship God. Jesus is the Messiah for the world, for all nations.

But didn't we earlier see in chapter 13 that the end (of the temple) doesn't come until the gospel is preached to the nations? And here in 15:37-39 the *end* is declared in and through Jesus' death. How are both these points correct? What hasn't yet been said is that Mark carefully uses two different words for temple. In chapters 11—13 he uses the word *hieron* which designates the physical structure, the building. In chapters 14—15, he uses the word *naos* which designates the sanctuary, the place where God and man meet (14:58; 15:29, 38; *except* 14:49 which refers back to the setting in chapters 11—13).

Jesus' death, then, is the end of the *naos,* the old sanctuary. But, the *hieron,* the buildings, still stand in Mark's time while the gospel is preached to the nations, until the end comes (13:10).

But is the *naos,* the sanctuary destroyed, never to rise again? What about 14:58 and 15:29? In three days I will *build another;* in John, *raise it up!* What else, according to Mark's Gospel, shall happen "in three days"? Do you remember? Do you understand!? The passion predictions were also resurrection predictions: "*In three days* I will rise again" (italics mine). By connecting the two events that will occur "in three days," Mark subtly but forcefully proclaims the resurrected

Jesus as the rebuilt temple, but located where?[10]

"But after I am raised up, I will go before you to Galilee" (14:28). And now for the second last verse of the book,[11] "But go, tell his disciples and Peter that he is going before you to Galilee; there you will see him, as he told you" (16:7). Did you discover what the meaning of Galilee is in your presession study? With what does Matthew 4:15 (quoting Isaiah 9:1) connect the term Galilee? Where will the raised temple be found? And for whom?

It is odd, and perhaps intentional, that the only other place Mark uses the term "three days" is in 8:2,[12] to describe how long the multitude on the *east* side of the Sea of Galilee waited for the bread of the Messiah. And, for whom was the feeding on the east side? *Seven* for *four* thousand with *seven* left over!

In Mark then, Galilee represents Palestine's open door to the nations of the world.[13] This call to world mission, which is inferred by Mark, is proclaimed openly by Matthew (28:16-20).

Mark's distinctive contribution lies in his correlation of the Gospel's major themes with Jesus' call to mission:

1. Both the temple will be rebuilt and the crucified Messiah will be raised *in three days,* and be met in Galilee! Hence, worship will be through Jesus, the new *naos*-temple who meets those who come for the call to make disciples of all nations.

2. Jesus as Messiah must die on a cross, a disappointment to Jewish political hope and an offense to disciples then and now who want only a sweet Jesus. Through such a death, akin to that of a political criminal, a Gentile affirms Jesus to be very Son of God, precisely in his obedient suffering and death. What a scandal! *God* disclosed—through a cross?!

3. Jesus is confessed to be Messiah of the kingdom only when Gentiles as well as Jews have been fed the messianic bread. Only then is the *secret* disclosed, with its truth

protected from nationalistic hope and anchored in following on the way, the way of the cross to God's kingdom, a way— for all nations!

> COME . . .
> die to the old,
> WORSHIP . . .
> through the new,
> PROCLAIM . . .
> to all nations.

Oh God,
  the old and the new,
  death and resurrection,
  religion and living faith;
All these tumble through our minds
  and we wonder
  just where we stand
  in relation to the cross.
Would I have identified with
  the religious leaders,
  Judas,
  Pilate,
  the crowds,
  Mary of Bethany,
  the disciples,
  the women, or
  the centurion?
Lord, who am I, anyway?
Where are my loyalties?
In which temple do I worship?

Please, Lord, focus my eyes on Jesus, Son of God,
  who died and lives
  for all nations
Lead me in the kingdom way.

> *Amen.*

STRUCTURAL DIAGRAM OF MARK 14-16

JESUS' DEATH AND RESURRECTION

Preparation for Jesus' Death	Peter's Denial	Arrest and Jewish Trial	Roman Trial	Crucifixion	Burial	Resurrection
14:1 14:25	14:26-31	14:32 14:65	15:1 15:15	15:16 15:39, 41	15:42-44	16:1 16:8
	(66-72)	young man (14:51, 52)	(those who stand by)	the women (15:40, 41)		young man (16:5) women (16:1-8)

Two Levels of Preparation

Betrayal (1-2, 10-11, 17-21)–Denial
Jesus (3-9, 12-16, 22-25)   (32-42)

Examples of Interchange of Two Themes

1. The two levels of preparation
2. Peter's promise and denial with the arrest and trial

Key Themes

Betrayal (*paradidomi*)
14:10, 11, 18, 21, ─────────── 41, 42, 44 ─────── 15:1, 10, 15

Who Is Jesus?

─────────── Messiah (14:62)── King of ── Son of
                    Son of Man   the Jews   God (15:39)
                                 (15:2, 8, 12)

The *temple* sanctuary (*naos*) ended

──────────────── 14:58──────── 15:29──────15:38

The *temple*, Jesus, for all *nations* (*ethnē*)
─14:9──────── 58─────────────── 15:39────── (16:7, 8)
       (28)   (Galilee)
       Galilee

Reflection, Discussion, and Action

1. Discuss this statement: Mark's secrecy explodes at the foot of the cross on the lips of a Gentile.

2. The Passion story has many persons in it who play different roles. Note the roles of the "young man" and "the women." On a line continuum, list all persons or groups of persons, from those most faithful to those most hateful toward Jesus. With whom do you suppose you would have identified had you been there?

3. What aspects of the passion story, and especially Mark's emphases, are most important for you and your congregation? Are we old temple people or new temple people? Is our view of Jesus' power rooted firmly in the cross?

4. As you reflect upon the temple theme in these last two lessons, what is its significance for the national and international character and loyalty of the church?

5. Several years ago when I was in Israel and took a course on the archaeology and geography of Palestine, I faced a final exam question as follows: What is the theological significance of the difference in the geography between Judea and Galilee? What do you think I wrote? I remember noting with amazement that, yes, David lived in the *closed in* hills of Judea and ruled from the well-defended, isolated mountain of Jerusalem, but Jesus grew up in Nazareth and preached in Galilee, areas *open to* the currents of world travel. And so, in God's providence, the difference between Judaism and Christianity! Discuss the view of Will Herberg, a notable Jewish theologian, that Christianity is Judaism's missionary department.

6. When we think of the meaning of Jesus' death, we usually think first of his dying for our sins. Is this emphasis found in Mark? What does Mark stress as the meaning and significance of Jesus' death? To what kind of action should that lead us? How is this related to being "born again," a phrase from John 3?

7. In what practical ways (use of money, time, friendships) are you living out the gospel *for all nations*— In short, are you a missionary?

Chapter 11

The Gospel of Mark: Summary and Significance

Presession Study

1. Your best preparation for this last study will be reading again the Gospel of Mark in light of what you've learned through this study.

2. Notice especially both the abrupt beginning and end (16:8) to the Gospel. How does this contribute to the mood of urgency in the Gospel? What other themes help to create this same effect?

3. List the *main* themes or distinctive emphases of the Gospel. Write a brief essay in which you show how these themes are interrelated in achieving Mark's purpose in writing the Gospel.

4. What is the meaning of the word "Gospel"? Look it up in a Bible dictionary or encyclopedia. From a concordance can you find how many times Mark uses the word? Note especially 1:14, 15. In what way(s) do these statements contribute to our understanding of the terms "gospel" and "a Gospel"?

5. Throughout this study we observed how certain sections of the Gospel have specific settings or geographical-topographical locations. Do you see any overall pattern? What is the setting (location) in which each section begins or as a total unit takes place? Any significance?

6. What is the relationship between Jesus' mission and the Jewish religion? How are Judaism and Christianity interrelated?

7. Based upon what you've learned in this study, how would you describe the purpose of Mark's Gospel? Why and when do you think it was written? To whom was it addressed?

EXPOSITION

The Beginning and Ending of Mark

"The beginning of the gospel of Jesus Christ, the Son of God" (1:1). Each of the six nouns in this opening verse contains sufficient meaning for an entire chapter. This study, however, has already spoken to the significance of the terms Jesus Christ and Son of God. Hence, this discussion will focus on the phrase, "the beginning of the Gospel."

Is the verse a title for the whole Gospel, for the Prologue only (vv. 1-13), or for verses 2, 3 only? The word, *beginning,* raises this question. Where does the *beginning* end? While a few commentators apply the verse as a title only to verses 2 and 3 (hence the prophetic anticipation is the beginning) and more relate it to the prologue (vv. 1-13), numerous scholars suggest that the verse functions as a title for the whole Gospel. Mark wants us to see that the whole Gospel is the *beginning.* We then may properly ask, The beginning of what?

But, first, let's note the meaning of the word *beginning.* The Greek word *archē* carries the idea of the first model (as in archetype) as well as that of coming first temporally. This insight provides two edges of meaning for the question, The beginning of what?

What does the Gospel as a book tell us? Do we derive from it a model or pattern for us to follow? Do we discover a temporal beginning for a new thing?

First, let's consider the Gospel as a model for proclaiming the gospel of God, the good news of the kingdom (1:14, 15). The Gospel is indeed both a model for what gospel we proclaim as well as a record of how the gospel began. The proclamation begun by Jesus continued through Mark's time, and later church history, and it still continues today. In fact, Mark no doubt intended to present the (temporal) beginning as a model in order to rally the Christians of his day to continue the work.

But what is the work, according to Mark? The work requires correct *understanding* of who Jesus is. Otherwise there is no gospel. It requires an understanding which confesses Jesus to be the Christ, the long-awaited Messiah. But it also requires an understanding that repudiates Peter's messianic politics (8:32, 33), a politics which would secure the messianic kingdom for Jews only, crushing other powers and peoples. It also requires an understanding that does not base Jesus' divinity primarily upon his miracles, but rather affirms him "Son of God" in the context of his faithful obedience, his suffering, and his death (15:39). And, finally, it requires an understanding that we too must take up the cross and follow the way of the Servant-Messiah.

This understanding then leads to *doing* the work, the work of "going to Galilee," participating in Jesus' mission to include all people in God's kingdom. It is the task of being the good news and spreading the good news to all people. The healed Gerasene demoniac must "go home," but only because his home is already where the mission is, among the Gentiles.

So it is fitting indeed that the Gospel ends at 16:8! For in this way, the Gospel's final punch line combines the message that Jesus is risen with the missionary face of discipleship, but all solidly rooted in the cross of the Servant. The Gospel tells and shows the beginning, but the work goes on. It calls you and me to join the ranks, and in this way we too shall be made to "become fishers of men" (1:17).

The Gospel leaves us with a picture of discipleship begun, but not completed. Each of the first three sections begins by focusing on the disciples—the call (1:16-20), the appointment (3:13-19), and the commission (6:7-13); the fourth section (8:27—10:52) majors on teaching discipleship; and the final sections educate the disciples on the missionary meaning of the gospel. Discipleship ranks as a predominant theme of Mark's Gospel.

But, the Gospel never tells us explicitly that the disciples ever fully understood. Even the women, who in many respects portray faithfulness to Jesus, end up frightened and fail to carry out "the young man's" commission (16:8). Hence the Gospel shows us the direction of discipleship, but does not close the challenge. It leaves it open for them, and for us! The Gospel ends with a call for us to *come, help,* and *finish* the mission begun by Jesus, the Christ, the Son of God.

The Main Themes of the Gospel

I hope your list is already complete from question 3 in the presession study assignment. How well does it match the following?

1. *Who Is Jesus?* The entire Gospel both poses the question and provides answers. But the first eight chapters especially (up to 8:27) build the question. Then all that follows answers the question from different perspectives, most notably, the Messiah of the cross and the Messiah for all people. The meanings of the various titles—Son of man, I AM, Messiah, Son of David, and Son of God—are all part of the Gospel's dramatic unfolding of the good news about Jesus. The truth of the drama bursts forth upon the reader through the voices from heaven at Jesus' baptism (1:11) and transfiguration (9:7), the cries of the demons (1:24; 3:11; 5:7), the "who" questions (4:41, 6:2-5), the *ego eimi* epiphanies (6:50; 14:62), Peter's confession (8:29), Bartimaeus' cry (10:47), and the Gentile centurion's confession (15:39).

2-3. *Understanding and Discipleship.* I put these two themes together because the disciples are those expected to understand. In 4:1-34, 6:30—8:26, and 8:30—10:52 Jesus wants the disciples to catch on, to discover who he really is. But they never fully learn. See 10-11 below.

4-5. *Secrecy and Mission to the Gentiles.* I choose these next because, as I see it, the secrecy emphasis, so striking in Mark, is correlated with respective responses. The Jewish leaders who rejected Jesus, exiling him from the synagogue (2:1—3:6), didn't even hear the proclamation of the kingdom ("even what he has will be taken away," 4:25b). To the Jewish people as a whole the gospel came in parables which they didn't understand (4:11b). To the disciples (also Jews) Jesus explained the teaching (4:34) but they also never fully understood. Only the Gentiles show fully positive response (5:18-20; 7:24-30) and clear perception (15:39). And only after the resurrection is Jesus' gospel fully and firmly angled to the Gentiles (14:28; 16:7). Hence, also, the secret cannot be disclosed until after "the Son of man should have risen from the dead" (9:9).

The secret can be told when those who hear understand!

6-7. Jesus' Passion and the Way of the Cross. Jesus' passion casts its shadow over the entire Gospel, not only in the sense that Jesus' death appears imminent, but also because the cross becomes the way for the disciple. These themes are intertwined with the five above. The christological question (who is Jesus?) turns out to be also a *Nachfolge—* way-of-the-cross question ("if anyone will come after me," 8:34). No room for idle curiosity! He who knows must respond in life!

8-9. The Kingdom of God and Its Urgency. All the above themes function as part of the Gospel's announcement: "The time is fulfilled, and the kingdom of God is at hand; repent, and believe in the gospel" (1:15). God's reign has begun; the kingdom comes in Jesus' coming. Hence, the urgency ("immediately, immediately"), the eschatological locale ("in the wilderness," especially 1:3, 4, and 13), and the inevitability of the kingdom's growth and triumph (4:1-34).

In the gospel's proclamation, then as now, the present becomes the edge of history, the opportunity for entrance into God's kingdom. And then a new history begins for us, one in which God's kingdom, though never fully manifested in history, is nonetheless realizing itself in the present community of the kingdom, the people of God.

10-11. Divine Action and Human Response. In these two themes I refer, on the one hand, to Jesus' divine power over all evil, crushing the power of the demons and restoring hope for the whole cosmos. On the other hand, I refer to the human response of "fear and amazement" found so frequently in the Gospel.[1] When Jesus unleashed the divine power, humans felt "fear," a term expressing both "trembling" and "reverence." But Jesus says, "Do not be afraid" (5:36; 6:50). Jesus not only conquers and overcomes but calls us to accept, without fear, the power of his divine presence. In Jesus, we encounter and are able to accept the divine presence.

In Mark it appears that fear and amazement function as the opposite response of understanding. If the disciples had *understood* about the bread, they wouldn't have been astounded (6:50-52). Again, when on the way to Jerusalem because the disciples didn't understand, they were afraid to ask further about Jesus' passion statement (9:32). Mark's final note, then, that the women ran away, afraid and trembling, (16:8) indicates that they, like the disciples throughout the Gospel, did not understand. Hence, in Mark's Gospel, only the Gentiles understand.

12. Unto All Nations. I enunciate this theme a second time (a second feeding?!). Mark's concern and Gospel beckoned the Christian believers of his day to join the mission of the kingdom. "The gospel must first be preached to all nations" (13:10). In the face of the imminent end of the temple and, indirectly, the end of the age, the call to bear testimony to the gospel for all people—even before kings and governors through persecution—took highest priority (13:9-11). And because the Gentiles responded positively—and thus, by inference, understood—the task ranked in highest importance; the resurrected Lord will meet you in "Galilee" (16:7).

I think that can be understood two ways in faithfulness to Mark's intention:

(1) there the resurrected Lord will lead you forth into his mission and

(2) there, as you respond to his mission, you will see the Lord of resurrection power. The whole world is Christ's parish, then and now, for Mark's first readers and for us.

The Structure of Mark: The Old for the New

In my doctoral study of Mark's Gospel, I observed that the Gospel is framed, as it were, with important images (or places) from Israel's Old Testament experience of salvation.

Look at the structural chart at the end of the exposition. Notice that each of the six sections begins with, or is punctuated with, a significant location, as follows:

—*The sea.* The first disciples are called by (and from) the Sea of Galilee (1:16-20) and this paragraph *begins* the first main section.

—*The mountain.* The disciples are made twelve on "the mountain" (3:13-19) and this paragraph *begins* the second section.

—*The wilderness.* The two main events of the third section occur in the wilderness (6:31-35; 8:4) and these events are intended to lead the disciples to understand who Jesus is.

—*The way.* The events of section four (8:27—10:52) happen as Jesus and his disciples walk "on the way" to Jerusalem and again discipleship functions as a major theme of the section.

—*The temple.* In sections five and six the temple (*hieron* and *naos* respectively) functions as a unifying, structural theme. While the disciples are not on center stage, the discourse about the end of the temple and the call to the Gentile mission (14:28; 16:7) are directed specifically to the disciples.

These observations led to the thesis that since scholars widely recognize the prominence of the discipleship theme in

Mark and the Gospel's structural division into these six sections, these particular places or settings may indeed be significant.

In my earlier biblical studies I had learned that the Old Testament story of salvation (in German, *Heilsgeschichte*) focused on certain specific events and periods of time in Israel's life as a people. In these events God acted to save his people.

I had also learned that though Israel traced its beginning back to God's call of Abraham (Genesis 12—35), the historical continuity of the people *as a people* began with their deliverance from Egypt and God's victory through the sea. The *sea* was the point from which Israel dated its beginning as a people.

God then led Israel to a *mountain,* Mt. Sinai, and there he provided the foundation for the life of the people as a nation—the Torah by which to live as well as the structure of the twelve tribes.

Then God sustained his people in the *wilderness.* He fed them manna from heaven, disciplined them, and taught them his ways (Psalm 78).

God had promised to send his angel to guard them *on the way* to the promised land (Exodus 23:20). God would fight for them on the way as he did at the sea (Exodus 14:14) and would lead them to the land of promise.

Once in the land and settled, the life of the people was focused for many years on the *temple,* promised to David (2 Samuel 7) and built by Solomon as his crowning accomplishment (1 Kings 6—9). Proper worship and use of the temple became a leading issue and point of tension between the kings and the prophets, between the priests and prophets, and between the people and God. Read Jeremiah 7.

One day the temple fell and Israel went into exile. Out of the midst of Israel's brokenness, prophet Isaiah proclaimed the *Lord's* purpose—for Israel to become "a light to the na-

tions, that my salvation may reach to the end of the earth"
(Isaiah 49:6; see also 42:6).

Why did I tell you this story? Because, I propose, it functioned as a model (an *arche*) for Mark's Gospel of Jesus
Christ, the Son of God. The new salvation story, the gospel of
the kingdom, is framed with the treasured images of the old
story. Jesus, the true Israelite, brings the old salvation drama
of sea, mountain, wilderness, way, temple, and nations to
fullness. Hence, as in Israel's history of salvation, so in
Mark's Gospel, the sea (1:16-20), the mountain (3:13-19), the
wilderness (6:31-35), the way (8:27—10:52), and from the
temple to the nations (11:1—16:8) mark out the successive
stages of God's salvation for all people in Jesus Christ. In him
we find the new beginning (*arche*), both in time and pattern.

The Purpose and Function of the Gospel

Mark's role in the early church as a mediating figure
between Peter, early leader of the Jewish Christians in
Jerusalem, and Paul, pioneering missionary to the Gentiles,
may now be seen as the life context out of which the Gospel
arose. As Ralph P. Martin has suggested, Mark's Gospel was
written as a handbook for continuing the Gentile mission
begun by Paul.[2] Paul's preaching scarcely referred to Jesus'
earthly ministry, but focused on his death and resurrection.
To prevent wrong understandings of Jesus and aid correct
ones, Mark wrote about Jesus' deeds and teachings from the
viewpoint of the cross and resurrection.

The Gospel's major emphasis upon the cross likely depends upon at least three factors. One, from the time of Jesus
to the time of Mark's writing the Gospel, the cross was
central to Christian belief and life. Two, just as Peter wanted
a politically imperious Messiah (8:32, 33) so Christians later
on, especially Gentile Christians, having orally heard the
stories of Jesus' miracles, may have tended to emphasize
Jesus' superhuman powers, as in the miracles, at the expense

of keeping central Jesus' suffering and cross.[3] And third, when the Gospel was written, the cost of identifying oneself as a follower of Jesus, the Christ, included persecution and sometimes martyrdom. Hence, the Gospel called Christians to faithfully persevere even at the cost of death.

Mark wrote the Gospel, likely in Rome, shortly before or after Peter's death around AD 65 (in Nero's reign) and only a few years before the temple's destruction in AD 70. See Appendix, I, Section A. With a little imagination, I can see John Mark, a man of zealous Jewish background with strong commitment to the Gentile mission, shuttling back and forth between Peter's and Paul's prisons in Rome with the express purpose of writing the story of Jesus, learned from Peter, and shaping it under God's guidance to serve the ongoing missionary task begun by Paul.

Because Paul's preaching could be too easily severed from Jesus' historical life, Mark took care both to proclaim the *earthly* deeds and teachings of Jesus and to anchor the story of Jesus in Israel's Old Testament history of salvation. In this way, under the inspiration of God, "the root out of dry ground" flowered for all nations.[4]

Mark, the Gospel of Jesus Christ, the Son of God, rooted in the old salvation history, blossoms with the new, Jesus and the kingdom of God—for all nations. The Gospel sets Jesus, the new temple sanctuary in the midst of the nations.

WINESKINS BURST ASUNDER
WITH NEW WINE!

Oh Lord,
*   what a journey we've taken together*
*   in the Gospel you've given us through Mark, and*
*   through the help of our teachers.*
We thank you for the good news of the kingdom
*   and for Jesus, your faithful Son.*
We thank you also for your salvation-purpose
*   in and through Israel, and*
*   for the continuity between*
*   the old story and the new story.*
We want to be "new wine" people,
*   filled with the Spirit of power,*
*   inspired by your kingdom of love, and*
*   oriented to "Galilee"—for all nations.*
Help us, Lord, to follow the way
*   of your holy Servant, Jesus,*
*   to take up the cross,*
*   to become as a child, and*
*   to live the servant life.*
May our security rest not in ourselves,
*   in this world's riches, or*
*   in this world's power,*
*   but in the power of the cross and resurrection.*
*   Amen.*

DIVISION I

THE STRUCTURE OF THE GOSPEL OF MARK

Title	Keynote Summary		Jesus' Authority				Kingdom Growth and Power				Messianic Disclosure					
		Introduction	*Section 1*	Day's Activity	Leper	Conflict Stories	*Section 2*	Para-bles	Mighty works	*Section 3*	Feeding Cycle 1	Bread and Understanding Responses		Feeding Cycle 2	Blind Man Healed	The Great Confession

Gospel | 1:1 | 2,3 | 4 | 13 | 14, 15 | 16-20 | 21 | 39 40-45 | 2:1 | 3:12 | 3:13-35 | 4:1 | 34 | 4:35 | 6:6 | 6:7-29 | 6:30 | 56 | 7:1 | 23 | 24 | 37 | 8:1 | 21 | 22-26 | 27-30

Jewish Gentile

Wilderness (3, 4 13 ------- 35 45)

Spirit (8, 10, 12 --------- 28-30)

Call of Four ———— Making of Twelve ———— Mission of Twelve ———— Disciples' Confession

Sea (thalassa) ———— Mountain (oros) ———— Wilderness (erēmos) ———— (8:4)

DIVISION II

The Way of the Cross (Discipleship)
to the Kingdom of God

Jesus: Judge of Exclusivism

Jesus: Messiah for the World

The Great Confession	Passion Cycle 1	Preview Kingdom Power	Passion Cycle 2	The Cost of the Kingdom	Passion Cycle 3	Bartimaeus	Temple Claimed, Cleansed	Temple Tenants Condemned	Destruction of Temple	Jesus' Betrayal	Crucifixion and Burial	Resurrection
8:27-30	8:31 38	9:1 29	30 42	9:43 10:31	32	45	11:1 33	12:1 44	13:1 37	14:1 15:15	15:16 47	16:1 8

Way (hodos)
(27 —————————————— -33, 34 ————————— 17 ——————— 32 —————— 46-52)

Passion Cycles: Each Time
—passion prediction
—disciples don't understand
—Jesus teaches discipleship

Temple (hieron)
(11, 15, ————— 35 ————— 1, 3 ——)
15, 16
27

Temple (naos)
(58 —————— 29—38)
—————————————(49)

Galilee
(14:28 ——————————— 16:7)

Way (hodos) ————————————————

Temple (hieron)
for all nations (ethnē) ——————————————

Temple (naos)
"in three days" in Galilee ————————————————

Reflection, Discussion, and Action

1. Can you visualize the Gospel as a whole? Without looking, can you recite titles for each of the six sections and relate each section to the locale which ties the story of Jesus to Israel's former story of salvation?

2. Within ten seconds can you cite six of Mark's main themes? If you didn't write an essay in the presession study (question 3), do it now. Or perhaps you'll want to write a second one.

3. What is the most important insight you learned from this study? What response does that insight require if you are a faithful disciple?

4. Do you have the gifts and abilities to be a missionary in helping others study the Bible? Could a few of you together begin a Bible study in your home, invite in neighbors and friends, and thus help others on the way to the kingdom?

5. Take time for silence and meditation. Ask yourself, What attitudes and priorities in my life need to be changed? Am I, like John Mark, using my gifts, even through stormy experiences, to help Christ's kingdom and cause?

6. Another focus for meditation: Which group of people in Mark's Gospel do I identify with? Read again the first part of chapter 2.

7. Write here the burden or promise of your heart:

Whose Way Leads Through a Tomb

CHORIC

Who is this man

> God-man
> man-God
> touching earth with spirit
> breathing heaven
> into clods
>> whose very word
>> becomes flesh

whose touch breath word

>> grows into leaping limbs
> what new order this
> in which
>> forms give way
>> to need
> and

>>> worth of person
>>> shatters dogma?

>> who
>> is
>> this man
> bursting the old wineskins
> of tradition
> the holy vessels of centuries
with his new wine
> the wine of freedom
> spirit rending flesh
> with kingdom newness
splitting the shapes
> of predictability
tearing apart the fabric
> of religious respectability
splintering the venerable frames
> of suitability

spirit *dunamis*
    EXPLODING
        from the inner core
        of Godness
        in the flesh

who is this man

           God-man
           man-God
       whose way
       leads through a tomb
           whom life
           could not contain
           whom the grave
           could not hold
spirit *dunamis*
    EXPLODING
        from the inner core
        of Godness
        in the flesh
a new day
        rolling back the darkness
a new kingdom
        sweeping crumbling forms into the dust
a new king
        ruling as Lord of all;
     crumbling dynasties
           clawing for lost power
           fading
               like fog
           —rolled back by heat
               of morning sun

        (Collage of sound—Sub-Voce.)

into the dust into the dust into the dust into the dust

           —From *To Walk in the Way*

CONCLUDING REMARKS

This may have been your first opportunity to study one book of the Bible in depth. I encourage you to continue this endeavor. The books listed in Section E of Appendix II will help you in this process. Wald's, Jensen's, and Martin's are helpful, especially for beginners; Yoder's (1982) and Virkler's are excellent guides for Bible study method to follow up this study.

A final note of information about this study is, perhaps, in order. Almost all the points made in this study may be found in one form or another in various books or articles on Mark. The main themes as described in chapter 11 are widely accepted by various scholars and noted by numerous writers. My interpretation of chapters 6:30—8:26, correlating together the *two* feedings, the *two* types of response in chapter 7, and the *two*-touch healing of the blind man with the respective Jewish and Gentile responses to Jesus, supported in turn by proposing symbolic significance in the numbers "five and twelve" and "four and seven," is found more rarely in commentaries and scholarly studies. The association of the two feedings with the Jews and Gentiles respectively (sometimes interpreted as reflecting Mark's contemporary eucharistic concerns) has been recognized by sqme writers (e.g., V. Taylor, A. Meyer, and Sundwall), but my interpretation of the numbers is found, as far as I know, only in John Bowman, *The Gospel of Mark: The New Christian Jewish Passover Haggadah* (Leiden: E. J. Brill, 1965), p. 176.

Similarly, one finds some recognition also of the significance of the *places* which, as this study proposes, function as the structural framework for Mark's Gospel. This recognition, however, is only in isolated, unconnected, or partial forms. Paul Minear, e.g., recognizes the motif-significance of the mountain, the wilderness, and the way.[1] Eduard Schweizer, among others, picks up Mark's temple-emphasis in

chapters 11—16, using the title "The End of the Temple of Israel and God's Turning Toward the Gentiles."[2] Dorothy M.
and Gerald H. Slusser have proposed that Jesus' call *from the
sea* (1:16-20) echoes Israel's salvation from and origin at the
sea.[3]

But for the first time in published form, as far as I know,
this study correlates these five or six redemptive motifs of sea,
mountain, wilderness, way, and "from temple unto the nations" with the structure of the Gospel and the already widely
recognized Markan emphasis on discipleship. Further, for
the first time in published form, this study proposes that
Mark's Gospel draws upon the place-sequences of the Old
Testament story of salvation for a structural pattern, a con-
ceptual framework for organizing the teachings and deeds of
Jesus' life and ministry. As such it proclaims God's good
news—the Gospel of Jesus Christ, the Son of God![4]

I hope these comments will help you sort out the more
commonly accepted insights from those newly proposed,
which, of course, need ongoing testing and evaluation both
by scholars and by congregational communities of faith.

Notes

INTRODUCTION

1. While these themes will be developed throughout the book, I summarize the main themes of the Gospel in ch. 11, pp. 198-200.

2. Philip Carrington, *The Primitive Christian Calendar: A Study in the Making of the Marcan Gospel* (Cambridge: Cambridge University Press, 1952), pp. 24-26, 90.

3. Clement of Alexandria described John as "a spiritual Gospel," so reports Eusebius in his *Ecclesiastical History* (Grand Rapids: Baker, 1962), p. 234 (Bk VI, Ch. XIV).

4. See Norman Perrin's account of the "The Rise and Fall of the Marcan Hypothesis" in *What Is Redaction Criticism?* (Philadelphia: Fortress Press, 1969), pp. 3-13.

5. *Ibid.,* pp. 7-9 and William Wrede, *The Messianic Secret* (German Original: 1901), trans. by J. C. G. Greig (Greenwood, S.C.: The Attic Press, Inc., 1971), pp. 229-236. See also Brian G. Powley, "The Purpose of the Messianic Secret: A Brief Survey" in *The Expository Times* LXXX, 10 (July 1969), pp. 308-310.

For a survey of interpretations of Mark's Gospel in recent history, see Ralph Martin, *Mark: Evangelist and Theologian* (Grand Rapids: Zondervan, 1973).

6. See Robert H. Stein, "The Proper Methodology for Ascertaining a Markan Redaction History" in *Novum Testamentum* 13 (1971), pp. 181-198.

7. Note the variety in interpretations of Mark's emphases in Joachim Rohde's summary, *Rediscovering the Teaching of the Evangelists* (Philadelphia: Westminster Press, 1968), pp. 113-152 and in "Mark's Gospel in Recent Research" by Howard Clark Kee, *Interpretation* XXXII, 4 (October 1978), pp. 353-368.

8. This work has been summarized well by David Rhoads in "Narrative Criticism and the Gospel of Mark," a paper presented to the Society of Biblical Literature in Dallas, Texas, November 1980.

9. This method is similar to rhetorical criticism as used and described by Phyllis Trible in *God and the Rhetoric of Sexuality* (Philadelphia: Fortress Press, 1978), pp. 9-22. I have also identified it with what Erhardt Güttgemanns calls Gestalt analysis; see Willard M. Swartley, *A Study in Markan Structure: The Influence of Israel's Holy History upon the Structure of the Gospel of Mark* (Princeton Theological Seminary, unpublished dissertation, 1973), p. 58.

10. For a summary and analysis of the structuralist contributions see Willard M. Swartley, "The Structural Function of the Term 'Way' *(Hodos)* in Mark's Gospel" in *The New Way of Jesus* ed. by William Klassen (Newton, Kan.: Faith and Life Press, 1980), p. 84, n. 3.

CHAPTER 1

1. Karl Heinrich Rengstorf, "ὑπηρέτης" in *Theological Dictionary of the New Testament,* Vol. VIII, p. 522.

2. Birger Gerhardsson, *Memory and Manuscript: Oral Tradition and Written Transmission in Rabbinic Judaism and Early Christianity* (Lund: C. W. K. Gleerup, Uppsala 1961), pp. 108-119, 243-244, See also Harold Riesenfeld, *The Gospel Tradition* (Philadelphia: Fortress Press, 1970), pp. 16-19, 54-55.

3. Kirsopp Lake and H. J. Cadbury connect Acts 13:5 with Luke 1:2 and suggest this interpretation also. See *The Beginnings of Christianity* (London: Macmillan, 1933), Vol. IV, p. 143. See also H. J. Cadbury, "The Knowledge Claimed in Luke's Preface," *The Expositor.* December, 1922, p. 414, n. 30.

4. J. H. Farmer, in *ISBE; Ed.,* James Orr (Grand Rapids, Mich.: Wm. B. Eerdmans Company, 2nd Edition, 1939), Vol. III, p. 1987. It would be textually and theologically more accurate to revise the last phrase of the second sentence to read: ". . . because he objected to the offer of salvation to the Gentiles apart from circumcision" (see Acts 15:1). Salvation was never offered "on condition of faith *alone*" (italics mine), unless faith is defined to include a changed life manifesting holy, obedient conduct.

5. *The Ecclesiastical History of Eusebius Pamphilus,* translated by Christian Frederick Cruse (Grand Rapids, Mich.: Baker Book House, 1962), Book II, Ch. XXV, pp. 79-80. Eusebius of Caesarea wrote in the fourth century AD.

6. The three men who visited Abraham (Genesis 18) are likely to be identified with the comment, "some have entertained angels unawares," in Hebrews 13:2. For extra-biblical references where an angel appears in human form (even as a *neanias* or *neaniskos*) and where humans appear in angelic form, see Robin Scroggs and Kent I. Groff, "Baptism in Mark: Dying and Rising with Christ," *Journal of Biblical Literature* 92, 4 (December, 1973), pp. 533-534 and 544 respectively.

7. The difference in numbers is more problematic; whereas Mark has one young man, Luke reports two men (24:4). Similarly, while Matthew reports one angel (28:2, 5), John reports two angels (20:12). While resolving these differences is difficult, Luke's and John's "two" may reflect the Old Testament background of certifying testimony through two or three witnesses.

8. Scroggs and Groff advance the view, however, that the *neaniskos* in 14:51 and 16:5 functions as a symbol of the Christian initiate. The loss of the linen cloth *(sindōn)* in 14:51 and the appearance of a white robe *(stolēn)* in 16:5 is said to parallel early Christian baptismal rites in which the initiate put off his old garment and put on a new robe *(stolē)* upon coming out of the water ("Baptism," pp. 540-543).

The weakness of this novel proposal is that Mark's emphases generally do not prepare the reader for the baptismal theme (as Scroggs and Groff admit in saying it is *"incompatible in and of itself* with Markan theological interests." p. 545). To argue as they do that this is Mark's subtle way of pointing "to the other side of that suffering" (p. 546), consistently stressed in the call to discipleship, is not convincing. Further, that two different Greek terms are used for the garment in 14:51 and 16:5 weakens the argument.

In an addendum, Scroggs and Groff note the relevance of Morton Smith's newly published thesis (regarding a *Secret Gospel of Mark)* that argues for an original Markan Gospel which contained a short section after 10:34 in which the term, young man *(neaniskos),* appears four times. This fragment, which despite Smith's view of its *original* status, almost certainly originated not before the second century (the view also of Scroggs and Groff). One might further propose that "this youth," the symbol of the baptismal initiate, is the only one in the Gospel who *understands* the secret of the kingdom (see chapter 11 below, points 2-5, 11-12 under "The Main Themes of the Gospel").

Were this the case (and I doubt that it is), then one could connect the symbol to the historical setting by regarding the Christian initiate as reflective of Mark himself (a view suggested by Winsome Munro in "The Feminine Presence in Mark's Gospel," unpublished paper read at the 1978 meeting of the Society of Biblical Literature, pp. 23-24). Hence Mark, via this symbolic figure, functions as the one who, because he understood the secret, directs the disciples to Galilee (16:7) and the Gentile mission, since as the Gospel discloses, Gentiles will understand. As this study will show, this view accords well with the Gospel's prevailing emphases and stands on its own merits (if one identifies the "young man" with the author, John Mark) apart from the symbolic baptismal interpretation of 14:51 and 16:5. This view also explains how John Mark was in a position of authority to write a Gospel which became widely influential in the development of the gospel tradition. While reference to oneself, as in 14:51 and 16:5, might appear self-imposing to us (compare the "beloved disciple" in John's Gospel), the *cryptic* reference is actually the opposite if indeed it reflects historical experience, an event which might have occupied several pages of impressive elaboration.

9. The first part of the quotation comes from Malachi 3:1 which in turn depends upon Exodus 23:20. That both quotations, the second from Isaiah 40:3, are ascribed to Isaiah indicates Isaiah's prophetic stature in the early Christian church, especially with regard to prophecies of messianic anticipation.

CHAPTER 3

1. The term "synoptic" literally means "eyed together." Matthew, Mark, and Luke are called the synoptic Gospels because they eye or view

the story of Jesus in much the same way. Unlike John they each present Jesus' ministry in a geographical framework of (1) Galilean Ministry, (2) Toward Jerusalem Ministry, and (3) Jerusalem Ministry. John records several trips of Jesus to Jerusalem with events and teachings in Jerusalem throughout the Gospel. Approximately 90 percent of the content in John's Gospel is not found in the Synoptics.

2. The RSV omits it. Both the 23rd edition of Nestles' and the 3rd edition of Aland's (UBS) Greek texts include it. Both manuscripts ℵ and B (as well as C*Δ 565) contain it. Although normally one would regard the second use as an accidental scribal redundancy, it's quite plausible that Mark intended special emphasis on this point and hence repeated it. Its omission then in some manuscripts, possibly by scribes who thought they were correcting a previous textual error, is itself an error.

3. Minear's comments on this text merit quoting:

> From this larger company of followers, Jesus had chosen twelve. At this point Mark gives us the roster of names (3:13-19). The place of the disciples' commissioning was significant—a mountain. In ancient oriental thought heaven and earth came nearest to each other on a mountain-top. The mountain was the place most appropriate for especially sacred revelations (9:2; 13:3), for significant appointments, for bestowals of grace and power. This was no casual or routine rendezvous. The Messiah had created a unique group for special duties. He had taken the initiative in selecting them, not because of their desires or capacities, but because of his plans for them.
>
> "He appointed twelve." The number was intentional. Jesus wanted new representatives of the twelve tribes of Israel. In a sense these men were to become the patriarchs of a new Israel. This appointment anticipated the later promise that they would sit on thrones, ruling the tribes (Matt. 19:28). The thrones were set around his throne, symbol of a shared authority. But this authority stemmed from his gift and training. For the time being they were to be "with him," learning the mysteries of God's new order. Then they would be "sent out" as Jesus' own delegates to the world, exercising his power to preach and to heal. He gave them new names, surnames, to signify this new role. Appointment, however, did not guarantee faithfulness. Even in this small number there was one "who betrayed him."
>
> There is much that escapes us if we read this naming of the Twelve without considering the Scriptures on which Mark and his readers had fed their minds. For example, Isaiah 43 should be carefully studied in this connection. In both passages, the Lord is creating Jacob and forming Israel, calling them by name because they belong to him (Isa. 43:1). He promises to be with them when they pass through the waters (vs. 14; compare Isa. 43:2 and Mark 4:35-41). He promises to gather sons and daughters from the end of the earth (Isa. 43:6), for they are to be his witnesses, his servants (Isa. 43:10). Yet in the time of Jesus, as of the

prophet, the salvation of God was rejected by the people "who are blind, yet have eyes" (Isaiah 43:8).—From *The Gospel According to Mark* by Paul S. Minear. Volume 17 of The Layman's Bible Commentary. © M. E. Bratcher 1972 p. 65. Used by permission of John Knox Press.

4. *The Parables of Jesus* (New York: Charles Scribner's Sons, rev. ed., 1963), pp. 13-18. While Jeremias' comments are valid if one is seeking to recover the possible meaning of the text as used by Jesus (since Jesus spoke in Aramaic) or in its Aramaic oral form before the Gospel, I nevertheless cannot agree that this is the proper interpretation of the text as it now appears in Mark. Certainly Mark knew what the Greek could and could not mean. The meaning of the text in its Greek canonical form must be sought elsewhere.

5. Mark's distinctive use of different demonstrative pronouns in the interpretation of the parable testifies to the correctness of this interpretation. In verses 15 and 16, to denote the seed that fell by the way and on the rocks, Mark uses "these" (*houtoi*), the *near* demonstrative pronoun; for the seed choked by the thorns, he uses the adjective "others" (*alloi*); but for the seed bearing fruit, he uses "those" (*ekeinoi*), the demonstrative pronoun specifying those further away. Matthew uses "this" (*houtos*) in all four cases and Luke uses "these" (*houtoi*) in all four cases. By these distinctions, Mark discloses his emphasis that the good soil is the Gentiles, those distant from the Palestinian setting of the parable.

6. Numerous manuscripts omit "Son of God" in verse 1. It is difficult to determine whether the original writing, the autograph, did or did not include it.

7. The voice at the baptism comes before the disciples are called and is addressed directly to Jesus, functioning as confirmation of power, preparing him for his ministry.

8. In Pennsylvania German the word is "dumbkopf" (someone who just doesn't catch on), a fitting description of the response of the disciples.

CHAPTER 4

1. This quotation from Eusebius, dependent upon Papias and in turn upon the Elder John of Ephesus, appears to contradict my reconstruction of John Mark's relation to Jesus in chapter 1 when it says that Mark neither heard nor followed the Lord. But that essentially is true also in my reconstruction. Mark came into touch with Jesus only indirectly during the last week of the Jerusalem ministry. Jerome's comment that Mark "himself did not see the Lord the Savior" is more difficult, but this one comment cannot be totally determinative of the conclusion. Specific information

such as this in the church fathers is not fully reliable as can be seen in the different views in the quotations on whether Mark wrote before or after Peter's death. The points that can be affirmed from the quotations are (1) Mark depended upon Peter's preaching for information about Jesus' deeds and words, (2) Mark did not set out to write a chronological biography of Jesus, and (3) the Gospel was written close to the time of Peter's death (c. AD 65).

2. *The Miracle Stories of the Gospels* (London: SCM Press Ltd., 1941), pp. 43-44.

CHAPTER 5

1. Mark 1:21-28; 5:1-20; 7:24-30; 9:14-30.

2. See John 6:70; 8:39-59; 14:30, 31; 16:33.

3. Since this text indicates that Peter was married and since Roman Catholic doctrine holds both that Peter was the first pope and that popes are to be celibate, the usual Roman Catholic interpretation of this text is that Peter's wife had already died or that Peter, upon his call to apostolic head, renounced his marriage obligations in order to fulfill his higher calling.

4. Willi Marxsen in his book, *Mark the Evangelist* (Nashville: Abingdon, 1969) devotes the first of his four studies to this Markan theme.

5. Ernest Best's study, *The Temptation and the Passion: The Markan Soteriology* (Cambridge: University Press, 1965) is helpful. The emphases of James M. Robinson in *The Problem of History in Mark* (London: SCM Press, 1957) and Ulrich W. Mauser in *Christ in the Wilderness* (London: SCM Press, 1963) also merit consideration.

6. *Temptation,* pp. 3-10.

7. *Wilderness,* p. 130.

8. *History,* pp. 27-39, Robinson stresses the eschatological nature of the combat as portrayed by Mark.

9. See Vernon McCasland's book, *By the Finger of God* (New York: Macmillan, 1951).

10. *The Devil Did Not Make Me Do It* (Scottdale, Pa.: Herald Press, 1977), p. 171.

CHAPTER 6

1. The first RSV edition translates: "They were distressed in rowing."

2. On your next reading of the Gospel note how often this theme occurs. For scholarly discussion of the "I AM" title in Mark (6:50; 13:6; 14:62), see John R. Donahue, *Are You the Christ?* (Missoula, Mont.: Society of Biblical Literature, 1973), pp. 92-93.

3. The Greek word, *pugmē,* is not translated by the RSV or KJV. Since it occurs nowhere else in the New Testament and rarely in other Greek literature, the meaning is unclear. "Up to the elbows" (RV) or "with the fist" are suggested meanings. Phillips translates it: "in a particular way."

4. Second Baruch 29:8. In *The Apocrypha and Pseudepigrapha of the Old Testament* R. H. Charles, Ed. (Oxford: Clarendon Press, 1913), Vol. II, p. 498.

5. Sib. Or. 7:149, *ibid.,* n. on v. 8. See also Isaiah 40:11, "He will feed his flock like a shepherd," and the similar expression in Micah 5:4.

CHAPTER 7

1. Luke's wording of Jesus' teaching seems to verify this interpretation, "But not so with you; rather let the greatest among you become as the youngest, and the leader as one who serves" (22:26). The term "youngest" denotes one who by definition is not great!

2. Chapters 9-11 will develop this point further.

3. For a better understanding of how to interpret the whole Bible from this point of view see Vernard Eller, *War and Peace from Genesis to Revelation* (Scottdale, Pa.: Herald Press, 1981) and Jacob J. Enz, *The Christian and Warfare: The Roots of Pacifism in the Old Testament* (Scottdale, Pa.: Herald Press, 1972). See especially chapter 6, "Turning Battle Songs into Hymns of Peace."

4. Minneapolis: Augsburg Publishing House, 1967.

5. The same preposition is used in 1 Corinthians 11:15 where the hair is given "for" (face to face) a covering. Not substitution, but *matching* is the idea. Compare "for" *(anti)* in "eye for eye, tooth for tooth" (Matthew 5:38).

CHAPTER 8

1. That Mark's use of "to enter the kingdom of God" depends upon the Deuteronomic phrase of entering into the land has been proposed by Hans Windisch, "Die Sprüche vom Eingehen in das Reich Gottes," *Zeitschrift für die Neutestamentliche Wissenschaft* xxvii (1928), 163-192.

2. *The Kingdom in Mark: A New Place and Time* (Philadelphia: Fortress Press, 1974), pp. 67-85.

3. "Kingdom and Parousia in the Gospel of Mark" (PhD dissertation, University of Chicago, 1970), p. 109.

4. For fuller treatment of the relationship between Mark 8:27—10:52 and exodus-symbolism, see my article (Swartley), "The Structural Function of the Term 'Way' *(Hodos)* in Mark's Gospel," in *The New Way of*

Jesus, ed. by William Klassen (Newton, Kan.: Faith and Life Press, 1980), pp. 73—86.

CHAPTER 9

1. Matthew and Luke do not mention Jesus' entry into the temple on Sunday evening (Matthew 21:10, 11; Luke 19:37-44).
2. This phrase was used by Amaziah, the priest of Bethel, in exiling Amos, the prophet (Amos 7:13). Like Amos, Jesus had little appreciation for such holy civil religion, as we shall soon see.
3. *Saint Mark (Layman's Bible Commentaries),* John Knox Press, 1962, p. 112.
4. The obverse side of the coin showed "a bust of Tiberius . . . adorned with the laurel wreath, the sign of his divinity." The legend read TI(BERIUS) CAESAR DIVI AUG(USTI) F(ILIUS) AUGUSTUS, meaning "Emperor Tiberius August Son of the August God." On the other side was the title PONTIF(EX) MAXIM(US), meaning high priest, with Tiberius' mother, Julia Augusta, sitting on the throne of the gods. The coin was "the most official and universal sign of the apotheosis of power and worship of the homo imperiosus (the Emperor) in the time of Christ" (Ethelbert Stauffer, *Christ and the Caesars,* [London: SCM Press, 1955], pp. 124-127).
5. Matthew, writing likely after the fall of the temple, expands Mark's one question (13:4) into three separate questions: the end of the temple, the sign of Jesus' coming, and the close of the age (Matthew 24:3). Luke, likely writing also after AD 70, mentions an age of mission to the Gentiles between the fall of the temple and the end of the age (Luke 21:24).
6. First Maccabees 1:54-61 and Josephus, *Antiquities,* Book XII, Ch. V, v. 4.
7. Josephus, *Antiquities,* Book XVIII, Ch. VIII. In AD 40 Emperor Gaius (Caligula) ordered the newly appointed president of Syria, Petronius, to war against the Jews and force them to erect statues to the emperor. The order was never carried out due to Petronius' delay and the emperor's early death.
8. Eusebius, the fourth-century Christian historian, gives us this information (*Ecclesiastical History,* Book III, Ch. V).
9. *Wars,* Book VI, Ch. IV, v. 4.

CHAPTER 10

1. Only in John's Gospel do we get information about the length of Jesus' ministry. His trips to Jerusalem for the annual Passover indicate a time-length between two and three or three and four years (depending on whether the feast in John 5:1 is a Passover).

2. The phrase comes originally from Martin Kaehler's writing in 1890, *The So-Called Historical Jesus and the Historic Biblical Christ,* trans. and ed. by Carl E. Braaten (Philadelphia: Fortress Press, 1963), p. 80, n. 11. Kaehler applied the phrase to the Gospels generally.

3. Considerable attention has been given to the Greek word *dei* in 8:31. It means "it is necessary" and carries the idea of an inherent necessity for the death of Jesus. Theologically, it is appropriate to connect it with God's providential purpose.

4. While living in a U.S. city, I witnessed backyard scraps between neighbor Catholic and Jewish boys. When something went wrong at play, the Catholic boys screamed, "I'm not going to play with you. You killed Jesus." The angry retort: "We didn't kill Jesus, you did!"

5. *The Gospel Message of St. Mark* (Oxford University Press, 1950), pp. 51-55.

6. What is the logical connection between the statement about the temple and Caiaphas' question, "Are you the Messiah?" One answer is "None," in which case no logical sequence obtains between verse 61a and 61b. Further, in that case one must ask how Caiaphas learned that Jesus claimed to be Messiah. Is that the secret that Judas betrayed?

Otto Betz, from his study of the Dead Sea scrolls, has proposed a logical connection between the temple charge and the messianic question, one which, in my judgment, is sound. Betz points out that the Essenes of Qumran had taken Nathan's prophecy to David in 2 Samuel 7:10-13 to mean that the messianic "Davidic king shall build a house for the name of God (7:13), i.e. the temple." Betz suggests that this association between the Messiah and his work, rebuilding the temple, played an important role in the eschatological hope of Judaism. Compare also the New Testament's frequent use of the stone (the Messiah) and cornerstone (of the temple?) text (Mark 12:10, 11 from Psalm 118: 22, 23). I agree with Betz in saying that "the fact that Jesus actually spoke the words about the building of the temple will hardly be seriously doubted. Six passages in the New Testament testify to it" (Mark 14:58; 15:29; Matthew 26:61; 27:40; John 2:19; Acts 6:14).

On this basis Betz correctly argues for a logical connection between the temple charge and the messianic question (*What Can We Know About Jesus?* [Philadelphia: Westminster Press, 1968], pp. 88-92).

7. In Matthew 26:64 the Greek term (*sou eipas*) is ambiguous. Jesus is noncommittal. It may be translated, "So *you* say," "So you *say*," or even "*You've* said it," implying ("*I* didn't"). Luke records the following (beginning with the question of the council): " 'If you are the Christ, tell us.' But he said to them, 'If I tell you, you will not believe; and if I ask you, you will not answer' " (22:67-68).

8. This is the view of Roy A. Harrisville in *The Miracle of Mark* (Minneapolis: Augsburg Press, 1967).

9. For more study of this point, read Hebrews 5:8, 9 and John,

chapters 5-8, especially 5:17-47; 6:38; 7:14-19, 28, 29; and 8:38, 39. Unlike Adam, Jesus in his full obedience to the Father fulfilled God's intention for humanity; thus, he is the second Adam, the perfect man.

10. For a list of commentators who have understood "the rebuilding of the temple" to refer to the Christian community, see Donald Juel, *Messiah and Temple.* (Missoula, Mont.: Society of Biblical Literature), p. 145; note Juel's discussion, pp. 143-158.

11. According to the majority of the earlier and more reliable manuscripts, the Gospel ends with verse 8 of chapter 16.

12. The phrase, "and in three days I will raise another made without hands," found in a few less reliable manuscripts at the end of 13:2, cannot be regarded as part of the original text.

13. For a summary of the scholarly work on the Gentile significance of Galilee, see G. H. Boobyer, "Galilee and Galileans in St. Mark's Gospel," *Bulletin of John Rylands Library* 35 (1953), pp. 334-338; and T. A. Burkill's essay on "Galilee and Jerusalem" in *Mysterious Revelation* (Ithaca, N.Y.: Cornell University Press, 1963), pp. 252-257.

CHAPTER 11

1. The most crucial texts are 4:41; 5:33, 36; 6:50; and 16:8. Significant also is the astonishment of the crowds (1:22, 27; 2:12) and the foreboding fear of the disciples (9:32; 10:32).

2. "A Gospel in Search of a Life-Setting," *Expository Times,* 80 (1969), pp. 361-364. See also Martin's excellent book, *Mark: Evangelist and Theologian* (Grand Rapids: Zondervan, 1972), pp. 161-162.

3. This emphasis has had significant support in Markan studies, especially in the form that Mark wrote to combat heretical opponents who made of Jesus a *theios-aner,* a divine man of wonder-working character. See Theodore J. Weeden, *Mark: Traditions in Conflict* (Philadelphia: Fortress Press, 1971). But this view goes overboard in following the current fad of suspecting "opponents" behind every New Testament book. The recent article by Robert C. Tannehill, "The Disciples in Mark: The Function of a Narrative Role," is an important corrective (*Journal of Religion* 57 [October 1977], pp. 386-405). This article argues against the "opponent" view and correctly emphasizes the primacy of the role of the disciples in Mark's Gospel and Mark's consequent purpose of promoting faithful discipleship in his time. His purpose continues to find fulfillment as *we* hear and respond to his call. This corrective is substantiated further by Jack Dean Kingsbury, "The 'Divine Man' as the Key to Mark's Christology— The End of an Era?", *Interpretation,* xxxv 3 (July, 1981), 243-257.

4. We should also remember that both Matthew and Luke used Mark in the writing of their Gospels, which highlights the cruciality of Mark's gift to the Christian church.

CONCLUDING REMARKS

1. *Saint Mark* (Layman's Bible Commentaries), John Knox Press, 1962, pp. 65, 82, 92.
2. *The Good News According to Mark,* trans. by Donald H. Madwig, John Knox Press, 1970, p. 229.
3. *The Jesus of Mark's Gospel,* Westminster Press, 1967, pp. 34-36.
4. For further exposition and development of these views see Willard M. Swartley, "A Study in Markan Structure: The Influence of Israel's Holy History Upon the Structure of the Gospel of Mark," unpublished doctoral dissertation, Princeton Theological Seminary, 1973. Copies are located in the Eastern Mennonite College Historical Library (Harrisonburg, Va.), the Associated Mennonite Biblical Seminaries Library (Elkhart, Ind.), and the Speer Library at Princeton Theological Seminary. A microfilm or bound photocopy may be ordered from University Microfilms, Ann Arbor, Michigan.

One might rightly question whether this structural sequence is of Markan or pre-Markan origin, or whether the structure surfaces unconsciously in the gospel story from the *"cultural structure"* of Israel's holy history, the likely hypothesis of the current hermeneutical method known as structuralism (see Daniel Patte, *What Is Structural Exegesis?* [Philadelphia, Pa.: Fortress Press, 1976], p. 25). Or should such a phenomenon be explained by "divine inspiration"?

My own judgment on this matter is that since discernible Markan redactional purposes are clearly associated with the motifs of "way" and "temple," it is highly probable that the entire sequence of redemptive motifs is of Markan origin. By "Markan" I do not mean exclusively one person but the Gospel's author shaped and influenced by his community of faith, including, most likely, both the apostles Peter and Paul. Within this context of discernment and intention, the factors of unconscious cultural-historical archetypes and divine inspiration are certainly operative and formative (see Norman R. Petersen's recent proposal that the approaches of historical exegesis and structuralism belong together, *Literary Criticism for New Testament Critics* [Philadelphia, Pa.: Fortress Press, 1978]).

Appendix I

Historical References to John Mark

A. Early Church Quotations Regarding John Mark*

Papias (2nd century, Ephesis, as quoted in Eusebius of Caesarea's *Church History,* written in Greek in the fourth century).

And the Elder [John] said this also: Mark, having become the interpreter of Peter, wrote down accurately all that he remembered of the things said and done by the Lord, but not however in order. For neither did he hear the Lord, nor did he follow Him, but afterwards, as I said, Peter, who adapted his teachings to the needs (of the hearers), but not as though he were drawing up a connected account of the Lord's oracles. So then Mark made no mistake in thus recording some things just as he remembered them, for he made it his one care to omit nothing that he had heard and to make no false statement therein.

The Anti-Marcionite Prologue (Latin text, 2nd century)

. . . Mark declared, who is called "stump-fingered," because he had rather small fingers in comparison with the stature of the rest of

---

*Reprinted by permission from Vincent Taylor, *The Gospel According to St. Mark* (London: Macmillan, 1959), pp. 2-7.

his body. He was the interpreter of Peter. After the death of Peter himself he wrote down this same gospel in the regions of Italy.

Irenaeus (Greek text, 2nd century, Lyon)

And after the death of these, Mark, the disciple and interpreter of Peter, also transmitted to us in writing the things preached by Peter.

The Muratorian Canon (Latin text, 2nd century, likely Rome)

At some things he [Mark] was present, and so he recorded them.

Clement of Alexandria (Greek text, 2nd century)

When Peter had preached the word publicly in Rome and announced the gospel by the Spirit, those present, of whom there were many, besought Mark, since for a long time he had followed him and remembered what had been said, to record his words. Mark did this and communicated the gospel to those who made request of him. When Peter knew of it, he neither actively prevented nor encouraged the undertaking.

They say that, when the Apostle knew what had been done, the Spirit having revealed it to him, he was pleased with the zeal of the men, and ratified the writing for reading in the churches.

Mark, the follower of Peter, while Peter was preaching publicly the gospel at Rome in the presence of certain of Caesar's knights and was putting forward many testimonies concerning Christ, being requested by them that they might be able to commit to memory the things which were being spoken, wrote from the things which were spoken by Peter the Gospel which is called according to Mark.

Origen (Greek text, 3rd century, Alexandria/Caesarea)

And second, that according to Mark, who did as Peter instructed him, whom also he acknowledged as a son in the Catholic Epistle in these words, "She that is in Babylon, elect together with you, saluteth you, and Mark my son."

Jerome (Latin text, fourth century, Bethlehem)

Second, Mark, the interpreter of the Apostle Peter and the first bishop of the Church of Alexandria, who himself did not see the Lord the Saviour, but narrated those things which he heard his master preaching, with fidelity to the deeds rather than to their order.

Interpretive Note: While these sources cannot be harmonized in all details they do agree on (1) that Mark depended on Peter's preaching for the source of the Gospel tradition, (2) that Mark's purpose in writing was guided more by teaching/preaching concerns than by any notion of chronology or biography as such, (3) that the Gospel was written very close to the time of Peter's martyrdom, hence around AD 65, and (4) that Mark was not associated with Jesus during the period of Jesus' public (Galilean) ministry.

Although Jerome's statement disagrees with the reconstruction of John Mark's relationship to Jesus in Jerusalem during the last week, the unreliability of the early church quotations in details allows us to consider the reconstruction of reasonable probability.

B. Collected Quotations from Jack Finegan, *The Mark of the Taw**

Eusebius' **Church History** (fourth century)
And they say that this Mark was the first that was sent to Egypt, and that he proclaimed the Gospel which he had written, and first established churches in Alexandria (II. 16).
When Nero was in the eighth year of his reign AD 62, Annianus succeeded Mark the evangelist in the administration of the parish of Alexandria (II. 24).

Chronographies of Julius Africanus (probably third century and possibly used by Eusebius)
Year of Abraham 2058, Olympiad 205 Year 2, Claudius Year 2 [Anno Domini 42]: Peter the apostle, having first founded the church of Antioch, is sent to Rome.
Year of Abraham 2059, Olympiad 205 Year 3, Claudius Year 3, [Anno Domini 43]: Mark the evangelist and interpreter of Peter preaches Christ in Egypt and Alexandria.
Year of Abraham 2078, Olympiad 210 Year 2, Nero Year 8, [Anno Domini 62]: After Mark the evangelist, Annianus was ordained the first bishop of the church of Alexandria.
(From *Die Chronik des Hieronymus,* ed. by Rudolf Helm in *Die Griechischen christlichen Schriftsteller* ... (GCS), Eusebius 7, 2nd ed., pp. 179, 183).

Jerome (fourth century, Bethlehem)
Mark the disciple and interpreter of Peter wrote a short gospel at the request of the brethren at Rome embodying what he had heard Peter tell. When Peter heard this, he approved it and published it. . . . So, taking the gospel which he himself composed, Mark went to Egypt, and first preaching Christ at Alexandria, he formed a church so admirable in doctrine and continence of living that he constrained all followers of Christ to his example. . . . He

---

* © John Knox Press, 1972, used by permission, pp. 28-38, showing the evidence (which Finegan uses for his narrative in historical fiction) for John Mark's role in founding the Christian church in Egypt.

died in the eighth year of Nero and was buried at Alexandria, Annianus succeeding him (from *Lives of Illustrious Men,* 8).

Epiphanius (fourth century, Palestine and Cyprus)
After Mark wrote the gospel he was sent by the holy Peter to the land of the Egyptians (in *Panarion haer.* LI. 6, 10, GCS 31, p. 256).

Hippolytus (third century, Rome)
Mentions "Mark, the curt-fingered" (*Markos ho kolobodaktulos)* in *Refutation of All Heresies,* VII, 30.

Universal History of Agapius (Arabic, 10th century, Menbidj, Egypt)
Mark wrote the Gospel in Latin for the inhabitants of the great city of Rome.
Peter Cephas sent Mark the Evangelist to Alexandria and made him bishop of that city; he sojourned there for two years and died. He had for successor Annianus, whose episcopate lasted twenty-two years (in "Kitab al-'Unvan, Histoire universelle écrite par Agapius [Mahboul] de Menbidj, éditeé et traduite en Francais par Alexandre Vasiliev," in *Patrologia Orientalis* 7 [1911], p 482, fol. 11 v.; p. 494, fol. 17).
The "two" years is likely a copyist error. Finegan suggests that "twenty" years is the original reading. Compare this with the information from Julius Africanus above, a twenty-year period from Mark's arrival in Egypt until his death.

The Calendar of Abou'l-Barakat
"Barmoudah 30. Mark, evangelist, apostle" (Barmoudah is the Arabic for the Egyptian Pharmuthi; Pharmuthi 30 is our April 25). This is held as the date of Mark's martyrdom at a place called Bucolia, beyond Point Silsileh, on the Egyptian Mediterranean coast, Bucolia is now submerged in the sea (from "Le Calendrier d'Abou'l-Barakât; texte Arabe édité et traduit par Eugene Tisserant" in *PO* 10 [1915], 269).

History of the Patriarchs of the Coptic Church of Alexandria
(Arabic, 10th century using earlier Greek and Coptic sources.)

The first biography of the history of the holy Church. The history of Saint Mark, the disciple and evangelist, archbishop of the great city of Alexandria, and first of its bishops (Arabic Text edited, translated, and annotated by B. Evetts, I, *Saint Mark to Theonas* [300] *PO* 1 [1907], 135).

Acts of Mark or full title, *Martyrdom of the Holy Apostle and Evangelist Mark of Alexandria* (Greek ms., 11th century, but original in Alexandria in fourth century).

John Mark had a long nose, raised eyebrows, beautiful eyes, a bald forehead, and a heavy beard. He was of middle age, but still quick in action. He was continent in affection, and full of the grace of God (in Migne's *Patrologiae . . . graeca* 115, cols. 163-170).

* * *

According to the later traditions, Mark's body was stolen from Egypt in AD 827 and taken to Venice, Italy. The church in Venice greatly honored Mark also. Today's Piazzo of San Marco was named after the city's patron saint, John Mark. The Cathedral of Saint Mark in Venice is a great tourist attraction; likewise, the church of Saint Mark in Alexandria.

Appendix II

Resources for Bible Study

A. Interpreting the Bible*

The *ultimate goal* in interpretation is to allow the Bible to speak its own message with a view to worship and obedience. In many cases what a passage says is clear. Then, the task of interpretation is concerned with discerning at what points the message touches life. However, in some cases the meaning of the passage must first be determined by careful study.

Letting the Bible speak for itself under the *guidance of the Spirit* is not easy. Tendencies to impose our ideas and biases need to be set aside. For example, middle-class North Americans find it easy to disregard the perspective of any other racial, cultural, or economic view of the Scriptures. Although we will always read and study the Bible from our own point of view, knowing interpretations of others will aid responsible interpretation. While it is important, therefore, both to seek the guidance of the Spirit and to consider insights of others, personal Bible study will make use of the following sound methods:

1. *Observe carefully what the text says.*

This approach to Bible study is known as the *inductive method* of Bible study. Essentially this means paying careful attention to both the literary structure and context of a passage. This approach involves looking at words, sentences, paragraphs, and larger blocks of material, and asking questions such as who? what? where? when? and why? It means noting recurring themes, causes and effects, and relationships within the passage, as well as similarities and differences from other passages of the Bible. This approach to the Bible allows the conclusions to grow out of the text.

2. *Be sensitive to different literary forms.*

Because the Bible is made up of a variety of *literary forms,* responsible interpretation must respect the differences between narrative, parable, poetry, and discourse. Careful study will recognize the Bible's use of symbolism and imagery, striving to get the basic message without making it say more or less than it was intended to say. As various literary forms and images are understood, the puzzling features of the Bible often begin to make sense (as in the apocalyptic books of Daniel and Revelation). Thus the Bible is seen as a living document bound up with the people of God and, as such, it is the message of God to and through His people.

3. *Study the historical and cultural contexts of the passage.*

It is necessary for us to take seriously the historical context of any given passage and the Bible as a whole. God revealed himself in history to a particular people over a period of many centuries. The written Word reflects the process of God's revelation of himself. Hence, faithful interpretation requires careful consideration of the historical context of any given passage. Much misinterpretation has resulted from disregard for the historical context of the passage being interpreted. A study of the Bible is always a study of a people. It is necessary therefore to enter the world of the Hebrew people and the people of the early church. This includes understanding their ways of thinking, their cultural pattern, and their distinctiveness amid the surrounding cultures and nations.

When we do that we can expect to experience a degree of cultural shock, just as we experience when we cross cultural barriers today. The ability to cross such barriers is one of the callings of the Christian, both to understand the Bible and to communicate it to other cultures of the present day. In order to understand the cultural, historical, and linguistic contexts of a given Scripture, the various *tools of biblical criticism* may be helpful. . . .

4. *Make wise use of various translations.*

In addition to taking seriously the cultural context of the Bible we must understand *the language itself.* Today we read the Bible in our native language. The Bible, however, was written mostly in Hebrew (Old Testament) and Greek (New Testament). In recent years many translations and paraphrases of the Bible have become available. These attempt to use contemporary English and some take account of better knowledge of ancient languages and manuscripts. A comparison of alternate renderings of a passage may lead to a clearer understanding of the biblical text. A knowledge of the biblical languages is necessary to evaluate the different translations of a verse. In general, versions made by committees (such as KJV, ASV, RSV, NEB, NIV, NASB, JB, TEV—*Good News Bible)* are more accurate and reliable than are translations and paraphrases made by individuals (such as *Weymouth, Moffatt, Phillips, The Living Bible).* Most paraphrases are so free that they are unreliable for serious Bible study. . . .

5. *Consider how the text has been interpreted by others.*

The endeavors of the early church, the medieval church, the Reformers, and contemporary Christians to understand the Bible will be instructive to us. Bible commentaries and Bible dictionaries can be valuable resources. A study of how the New Testament interpreted the Old Testament will also be helpful. . . . By considering how . . . Christians throughout history have interpreted the Bible, we may be able to understand it more clearly.

6. *Consider the message of the Bible as a whole.*

One of the major errors in biblical interpretation is failure to relate a given passage of Scripture to the overall message of Scripture. It is therefore necessary to take seriously the message of the Bible as a whole and compare Scripture with Scripture. This requires acquaintance with the unfolding drama of the Bible, its major themes, and how the various themes are related and integrated into a whole. The meaning of any part cannot be arrived at apart from the message of the whole. . . .

7. *Meditate upon the Word in the spirit of prayer.*

As we learn what the passage says and means, we should meditate upon its message. We should ask ourselves: In what way does this Scripture speak to my life and our lives? How does it instruct me and my fellow believers? How does it teach, correct, reprove, and train in righteousness (2 Timothy 3:15-17)? Some specific topics of the Bible may not apply directly to us today, although they may be pertinent to Christians in other cultures; examples are circumcision, eating meat offered to idols, and the Christian's relation to the ceremonial practices in the Old Testament. However, the manner in which God's people of the New Testament worked through these issues will be instructive to us today.

8. *Listen for the guidance of the Spirit, individually and congregationally.*

The Spirit gives life to the written Word. The Spirit uses the Word to convict of sin, righteousness, and judgment (John 16:7-11). The Spirit likewise leads us into the truth, guiding our perception of the written words (John 16:13). As new insights and convictions come through personal study, we should share and test them with other Christian brothers and sisters who are listening to the Spirit. The experience of the Spirit, the interpretation of the Word, and the understanding of the church should agree.

9. *Respond obediently to the Bible's message.*

Interpretation of the Bible must include our own response to its message. The response may be praise or repentance, thanksgiving or confession, examination of inner attitudes or restitution to one wronged. The Scripture speaks to us only if we are open to its message. Sin in our lives, such as malice toward other people, hinders us from wanting to know and hear the Scripture message (1 John 2:4-6; John 8:31 ff.; cf. Matthew 5:22, 23). Lack of love and commitment to one another will also hinder believers in their effort to arrive at unity in their understanding of the Bible. Through faithful responses to the Word, we discover the power of the biblical message to upbuild the interpreting community—"to break and to heal, to wound and to cure."

---

*Section C of Part I from *Biblical Interpretation in the Life of the Church,* a summary statement adopted by Mennonite General Assembly, June 18-24, 1977 (Scottdale, Pa.: Mennonite Publishing House, 1977). Copies of this complete statement are available from Mennonite Publishing House, Scottdale, Pa. 15683.

B. An Outline of the Inductive Approach to Bible Study*

I. Observation

   A. Structure

      1. Structural units

         phrase—several parts of speech constituting a partial (incomplete unit of thought)

         clause—a group of terms including a subject and verb, constituting a partial (or whole) unit of thought

         sentence—one or more clauses constituting a unit of thought

         paragraph—a group of sentences constituting a unit of thought

         segment—a group of closely related paragraphs constituting one central unit of thought

         section—a group of segments related to each other by one unit of thought

         division—a group of sections related to each other by one strand of thought, emphasis, or viewpoint

         book—a group of divisions related to each other by one purpose, emphasis, or viewpoint

      2. Structural laws of relationship

        a. Comparison—the association of like things

        b. Contrast—the association of opposites

        c. Repetition—the *reiteration* of the *same* terms

        d. Continuity—the recurrence of *similar* terms

        e. Continuation—the extension of one aspect into another sphere

        f. Progression—the arrangement of materials effecting movement from lesser to greater to greatest or vice versa

        g. Climax—the highest point of a progressive arrangement of materials

        h. Cruciality—the pivotal point which changes the direction of movement

        i. Means to end—the instrumental use of material to effect some ends

      j. Interchange—the alternation of compositional elements

      k. Particular and General—the movement from a particular to general or general to particular

      l. Cause and Effect—the progression from cause (problem) to effect (answer or result)

      m. Explanation—a stated idea or event followed by its interpretation

      n. Introduction—the background of ideas or events presented as preparatory to that which follows

      o. Summarization—a gathering together of the main idea into a concise statement or a literary rounding off of an idea or event

      p. Interrogation—the use of a question to effect answer, explanation, or portrayal of problem

  3. Structural raw materials

    a. Persons   Any one of these five "resources" may be

    b. Places   used via the "laws of relationship" to

    c. Time   give unity to the various "structural units"

    d. Events   in 1 above.

    e. Ideas

  4. Structural principles

    a. Selectivity (relative quantity)

    b. Grammatical selection (conjunctions, etc.)

    c. Literary arrangement

B. Terms (a given word bound to one meaning only by context and usage)

  1. Routine term—denotes words with routine use; does not need definition

  2. Nonroutine term ("strong" or "key")—denotes words which have special function or meaning

  3. Literal—denotes words with normal meaning

  4. Figurative—denotes words with derived meaning from usage in context (e.g. "shepherd" in Ps. 23)

C. Atmosphere

  1. Detected by words of emotion (sorrow, joy, suspense)

2. Disclosed by movement, style, or structure of passage
D. Literary form
  1. Discoursive or logical literature
  2. Prose narrative
  3. Poetry
  4. Drama or dramatic prose
  5. Parabolic literature
  6. Apocalyptic literature
II. Interpretation
  A. Interpretive questions
    1. Definitive phase
      a. *What* is the meaning of the nonroutine terms?
      b. *What* is the pattern of the structural relations?
      c. *What* are the characteristics of this literary form?
    2. Rational phase
      a. *Why* is this particular term used?
      b. *Why* does this structure occur?
      c. *Why* is this literary form and atmosphere used?
    3. Implicational phase
      a. What does the use of this term *imply?*
      b. What does this pattern of structure *imply?*
      c. What does this literary form or atmosphere *imply?*
    4. Specific passage questions
      a. Context?
      b. Addressee—addressor?
      c. Who? How? When? Where?
  B. Interpretive answers
    1. Determinants of interpretive answers
      a. Reader determinants (subjective)
        (1) Spiritual sense
        (2) Common sense
        (3) Experience
      b. Text determinants (objective)
        (1) Etymology, usage, synonyms, comparative philology, and kinds of terms
        (2) Grammatical inflections
        (3) Context and inter-text relations

                (4) Literary forms
                (5) Atmosphere
                (6) Author's purpose and viewpoint
                (7) Historical background
                (8) Psychological factor
                (9) Ideological factor
               (10) Unfolding revelation
               (11) Inductive view of inspiration
               (12) Textual criticism
               (13) Organic unity
               (14) Interpretation of others
     2. Formulation of interpretive answers—strive for a
             comprehensive, methodical, "aware" answer

III. Application
    A. Evaluation (timeless vs. dated value)
      1. Old Testament passages which were of a "foreshadow" nature or restricted in truth by virtue of an unfolding revelation
      2. Local situations or practices (circumcision, food offered to idols, etc.) as opposed to timeless principles
      3. Passages addressed to concrete historical situations but applicable to anyone
      4. Relationship of passage to central "salvation story"
    B. Application
      1. Analyze contemporary situation
      2. Apply the timeless aspects of the Bible to contemporary situations
        a. Theoretical vs. practical application
        b. Scope of application
            —personal and church community
            —local and national
            —economic and political
            —specific and universal

---

*Summarized and adapted by W. Swartley from Robert A. Traina, *Methodical Bible Study: A New Approach to Hermeneutics* (New York: Ganis and Harris, 1952).

C. A Suggested Sequence of Tasks and Questions Leading to Understanding of the Bible Text

1. Read and reread the passage.

2. Determine the structural limits: divisions, sections, segments, and paragraphs.

3. Break down the segment into paragraphs.

4. Give each paragraph a "descriptive content" title.

5. Observe structural laws of relationship between paragraphs and within paragraphs.

6. List the nonroutine terms, seeking to determine the specific meaning, significance, and implications of their usage.

7. Observe the significance of selectivity factors.

8. Discover the atmosphere of the passage.

9. Observe the kinds of literary forms employed.

10. Ask where, what, who, whom, when, and why.

11. Study the context. Seek to determine the function of this segment in the larger section.

12. Ask the questions of historical, cultural, geographical, and ideological background. To whom, by whom written or spoken?

13. Ask the interpretive questions. What does it mean?

14. What seems to be the central theme of the passage? What aspect, if any, of the passage is relevant only to the historical setting? What is applicable to today?

15. How do we apply this truth to our personal and community situations today?

D. Books Especially Helpful for Studying Mark

Recommended Companion Volume

Bender, Urie A. *To Walk in the Way.* Scottdale, Pa.: Herald Press, 1979.

Helpful Bible Studies on Mark

Harder, Helmut. *The Good News About Jesus Christ According to Mark: Leader's Guide.* Newton, Kansas: Faith and Life, 1975. A pupil's text of Mark (large print with wide margins and some pictures) is also available with this study.

Kinsler, R. Ross. *Inductive Study of the Book of Mark.* South Pasadena, California: William Carey Library, 1972.

Kunz, Marilyn and Schell, Catherine. *Mark (Neighborhood Bible Studies).* Wheaton: Tyndale House, 1977.

McCarter, Neely Dixon. *Help Me Understand, Lord: Prayer Responses to the Gospel of Mark.* Philadelphia: Westminster Press, 1978.

Rinker, Rosalind. *Who Is This Man? Studies in the Life of Christ from the Gospel of Mark.* Grand Rapids: Zondervan, 1962.

Smith, Thomas and Frances. *Jesus Alive: The Mighty Message of Mark.* Winona, Minnesota: St. Mary's College Press, 1973. Written for study in high school or college classes. A *Teaching Guide* (1975) contains suggested activities and questions.

Smith, Thomas and Frances. *Good News About Jesus as Told by Mark,* Winona, Minnesota: St. Mary's College Press, 1977. This book, designed for adult education seminars, is a condensed adaption of the 1973 volume. An accompanying *Guide for Group Leaders* (1977) is also available.

Whiston, Lionel. *Relational Studies in Mark,* Vols. I, II, III. Waco, Texas: Word Books, 1976. Introduces a method of Bible study suggesting ways of spiritual identification with the text.

Parallel Reading

Kelber, Werner. *Mark's Story of Jesus.* Philadelphia: Fortress Press, 1979. An enjoyable volume which contains numerous insights similar to mine. I disagree, however, with his view of the role of the disciples (see p. 222, n. 3).

Walters, Carl, Jr. *I, Mark: A Personal Encounter.* Atlanta: John Knox Press, 1980. A different, but helpful approach.

For More Advanced Study of Mark
(Begin with Starred Books)

Achtemeier, Paul J. *Mark (Proclamation Commentaries: The New Testament Witnesses for Preaching).* Philadelphia: Fortress Press, 1975.

Anderson, Hugh. *The Gospel of Mark (New Century Bible).* Greenwood, S.C.: The Attic Press, 1976.

Barclay, William. *The Gospel of Mark.* Edinburgh: Saint Andrew Press, 1954.

Burkill, T. A. *Mysterious Revelation: An Examination of the Philosophy of St. Mark's Gospel.* Ithaca, N.Y.: Cornell University Press, 1963.

Cranfield, C.E.B. *The Gospel According to Saint Mark.* Cambridge: Cambridge University Press, 1959. Assumes use of Greek.

*Finegan, Jack. *Mark of the Taw.* Richmond, Va.: John Knox, 1972.

*Harrisville, Roy A. *The Miracle of Mark.* Minneapolis: Augsburg, 1967.

Hiebert, David E. *Mark: A Portrait of a Servant.* Chicago: Moody Press, 1974.

Lane, William L. *The Gospel According to Mark (New International Commentary).* Grand Rapids: Eerdmans, 1974.

Lightfoot, R. H. *The Gospel Message of St. Mark.* Oxford University Press, 1950.

Martin, Ralph. *Mark: Evangelist and Theologian.* Grand Rapids: Zondervan, 1973. An excellent survey of the various scholarly attempts to interpret and understand Mark's Gospel in the last century, together with Martin's own view of Mark's purpose (see my reference to Martin in chapter 11 above). This book should be read after reading several of the starred volumes.

Meye, Robert P. *Jesus and the Twelve: Discipleship and Revelation in Mark's Gospel.* Grand Rapids: Eerdmans, 1968.

*Minear, Paul. *Saint Mark (Layman's Bible Commentaries)*. Nashville: Abingdon, 1962.

Nineham, D. E. *The Gospel of St. Mark (The Pelican New Testament Commentaries)*. Baltimore: Penguin, 1963.

*Schweizer, Eduard. *The Good News According to Mark*. Richmond, Va.: John Knox, 1970.

Slusser, Dorothy M. and Gerald H. *The Jesus of Mark's Gospel*. Philadelphia: Westminster, 1967.

Taylor, Vincent. *The Gospel According to St. Mark*. New York: Macmillan, 1959.

For Further Advanced Redactional Study of Mark

Belo, Fernando. *A Materialist's Reading of the Gospel of Mark,* trans. from the French by Matthew J. O'Connell. Maryknoll, N.Y.: Orbis Books, 1981.

Best, Ernest. *Following Jesus: Discipleship in the Gospel of Mark*. Sheffield, U.K.: JSOT Press, 1981.

Kee, Howard Clark. *Community of the New Age: Studies in Mark's Gospel*. Philadelphia: Westminster Press, 1977.

Kelber, Werner. *The Kingdom in Mark: A New Place and a New Time*. Philadelphia: Fortress Press, 1974.

Kelber, Werner, ed. *The Passion in Mark: Studies on Mark 14-16*. Philadelphia: Fortress Press, 1976.

Marxsen, Willi. *Mark the Evangelist: Studies on the Redaction History of the Gospel,* trans. by Roy A. Harrisville, et. al. Nashville: Abingdon, 1969.

Michie, Donald and Rhoads, David. *Mark As Story: An Interpretation of a Gospel*. Philadelphia: Fortress, forthcoming, 1982.

Perrin, Norman. "Towards an Interpretation of the Gospel of Mark" in *Christology and a Modern Pilgrimage: A Discussion with Norman Perrin,* ed. by Hans Dieter Betz. Claremont, Calif.: New Testament Colloquium, 1970.

Robinson, James M. *The Problem of History in Mark (Studies in Biblical Theology, No. 21)*. Naperville, Ill.: Allenson, 1957.

Weeden, Theodore J. *Mark: Traditions in Conflict*. Philadelphia: Fortress Press, 1971.

E. Recommended Books on Method of Bible Study

Gettys, Joseph M. *How to Enjoy Studying the Bible.* Richmond, Va.: John Knox Press, n.d. Gettys has over a dozen other volumes on specific books of the Bible.

Jensen, Irving L. *Independent Bible Study: Using the Analytical Chart and the Inductive Method.* Chicago: Moody Press, 1963. Jensen has published numerous self-study manuals on NT books.

Martin, John R. *Keys to Successful Bible Study.* Scottdale, Pa.: Herald Press, 1981.

Traina, Robert A. *Methodical Bible Study: A New Approach to Hermeneutics.* New York: Ganis and Harris, 1952.

Virkler, Henry A. *Hermeneutics: Principles and Processes of Biblical Interpretation.* Grand Rapids, Mich.: Baker Book House, 1981.

Wald, Oletta. *Joy of Discovery in Bible Study,* rev. ed. Minneapolis: Augsburg, 1975.

Yoder, Perry B. *Toward Understanding the Bible: Hermeneutics for Lay People,* Newton, Kan.: Faith and Life Press, 1978.

Yoder, Perry B. *From Word to Life.* Scottdale, Pa.: Herald Press, forthcoming 1982.

Author Index

Proper Name Index

Subject Index

Scripture Index

OLD TESTAMENT

NEW TESTAMENT

MARK: A. Index of Segments and Sections (indicates first where the segment/section is discussed as a whole and also where it is referred to in other chapters of the book)

MARK: B. General Index (references to verses within the section of each chapter's study are not included; see chapter noted above and find the discussion of the verse or paragraph which contains the verse)

Willard M. Swartley is director of the Institute of Mennonite Studies and Professor of New Testament at the Associated Mennonite Biblical Seminaries, Elkhart, Indiana. He teaches courses in biblical interpretation, New Testament theology and ethics, and war and peace in the Bible.

He holds the PhD degree from Princeton Theological Seminary and has studied at Garrett Theological Seminary and Tübingen University. He received the BD degree from Goshen Biblical Seminary and earned his BA degree at Eastern Mennonite College.

Swartley has published numerous articles, among which are "The Biblical Basis of Stewardship" in *The Earth Is the Lord's* (Paulist Press, 1978); "Politics and Peace *(Eirēnē)* in Luke's Gospel" in *Political Issues in Luke-Acts* (Orbis Press, 1982); "The Structural Function of the Term 'Way' *(Hodos)* in Mark's Gospel" in *The New Way of Jesus* (Faith and Life Press, 1980); and a scholarly essay on Ignatius in *Vigilae Christianae* (1973). In 1983 Swartley published an extensive hermeneutical study entitled *Slavery, Sabbath, War, and Women: Case Issues in Biblical Interpretation* (Herald Press).

Swartley served on the Mennonite Publication Board from 1971 to 1980 and was executive secretary for the Conrad Grebel Projects Committee, 1973-1980. He taught at Goshen College, Eastern Mennonite

College and Seminary, and Conrad Grebel College.

Willard and Mary (Lapp) Swartley are the parents of Louisa Reneé and Kenton Eugene.